UNIVERSAL DECIMAL CLASSIFICATION

A PRACTICAL PRIMER

V. V. V. SATYANARAYANA
Bharat Heavy Electricals Ltd.
Corporate Research & Development
HYDERABAD

Ess Ess Publications
4837/24, Ansari Road, Darya Ganj,
New Delhi-110002
✆ : 3260807

First Published 1998

First Reprint 2000

ISBN : 81-7000-240-0

Price : 600.00

Published by :

Ess Ess Publications

4837/24, Ansari Road, Darya Ganj,
New Delhi - 110 002
Phone : 3260807

Laser Typesetting :

CINOGRAPHICS

E-41, New Multan Nagar
New Delhi
Phone : 5583866

Printed at :

Print Line, New Delhi

CONTENTS

Preface

Classification of knowledge is very important especially in the age of knowledge explosion. Knowledge is growing at an exponential rate and without organising the knowledge it is very difficult to make use of that knowledge. Classification is the only technique to systematically organise knowledge and put the same to right use at the right time.

Many classification schemes have been in vogue for the last five decades. However, Universal Decimal classification scheme is unique in many respects when compared to the other schemes. It is supported by many experts who have formed as a consortium and have been looking after the process of keeping the scheme in tune with the latest developments in the universe of knowledge. It is therefore a live scheme.

Though Universal Decimal Classification scheme was introduced during 1920s, its practical use has not been that significant so far as Indian sub continent is concerned. This is partly due to lack of proper awareness of the scheme and also due to lack of practical guides that will help the users and the classification professionals to expose themselves to this classification scheme. It has been, therefore, felt that a practical guide was needed to make best use of this high utility classification scheme.

The present book is intended to act as a practical guide to the practitioners and as well as to the users of the libraries where this scheme is in use. It is not the intention of the author to present the theory of classification in this book. However, a brief account of the norms and characteristics of a classification scheme is given to refresh the readers mind with the foundation for classification scheme. Basic theory of Universal Decimal classification is thoroughly discussed with a view to make the reader appreciate the scheme to its simplicity and easy to use.

While each main class is analysed with the support of examples, each example is analysed tracing its hierarchy. Main classes, Subclasses, Main tables, Auxiliary tables and all components of the classification scheme have been extensively covered and thoroughly discussed in this book. 200 Worked out examples have been provided. These examples are selected to represent various main classes and their subdivisions. Use of auxiliary divisions is also represented in these worked out examples:

Many of the points made are derived from my experience over many years of working with the Universal Decimal Classification to classify books and other documents especially in science and technology areas. Classification process has been described and illustrated with the help of schematic diagram. It is hoped that the present book will act as a practical guide and as a workbook.

Throughout, examples of numbers and actual titles, published by various publishers, classified by the scheme are given to assist the classifier in a practical situation to be aware of the variations and alternative arrangements that may be expressed. Titles for practical examples are taken from American Books in print and other book selection tools. Considerable assistance has been derived from the Universal Decimal Classification schedules of various editions.

V.V.V.Satyanarayana

Introduction

Classification is a technique for systematic arrangement of knowledge. In classification, concepts are assembled according to the extant to which they are alike and are separated on a basis of the extant to which they are unlike. Systematic arrangement of knowledge has been necessitated due to the fact that the readers' time in search of information is to be saved. The classification scheme and its schedules should be devised in such a way that the users of classification scheme and the audience, to which the scheme is meant should be benefitted in a most appropriate manner. A classification scheme should reflect the contemporary knowledge of the subjects and their developments. Classification is necessary to understand various subjects in their proper perspective and to correlate one subject with the other in so far as their proximity is concerned. Classification is an universal phenomenon and hence it can be applied to any thing and everything in the world. Classification is an art when it comes to the classification of universe of knowledge involving various subjects. Sufficient knowledge is required to classify universe of knowledge. Each subject is derived from the universe of knowledge by applying classification principle. Hence the subjects are interdependent or interdisciplinary. Therefore one must be knowledgeable and careful enough to draw a line between various subjects. A classification is only a means to derive subjects from the universe of knowledge and not the end of knowledge itself. Classification has definite advantages in the organisation of knowledge, Physical location of documents, identifying the desired item in a vast resources of knowledge and in the ocean of knowledge itself. In the age of literature explosion and the growth of knowledge resources, classification is the only method to organise the subject content of the knowledge resources and provide retrieval mechanism to quickly locate the desired item in the vast resources spectrum. Library classification is as old as the inception of Library science itself. Library classification in particular has been defined as "the systematic arrangement by subject of books and other material on shelves or of catalogue and index entries in the manner which is most useful to those who read or who seek a definite piece of information". In other words, library classification serves a dual function: to arrange items in a logical order on library shelves and to provide a systematic display of bibliographic entries in printed catalogues, bibliographies and indexes. Examples can be attributed to many of the National Bibliographies published in the world.

In any collection of documents, the most appropriate basis for determining groups varies according to the needs of the collection. The needs here are user's needs. For example the groups can be by author, by physical form, by size, by date of publication or by subject. In modern library classification systems, subject is the predominant characteristic for grouping.

0.1 LIBRARY CLASSIFICATION

In the library context, classification as a term refers both to the development of schemes for the systematic display of all aspects of the various fields of knowledge and to the art of arranging books or other objects in conformity with such schemes. In other words, it is used both for creation of a classification scheme and for its application. People who are involved in creation of a classification scheme are classificationists and persons who apply such a scheme are classifiers.

Library classification is borrowed from the Philosophical principles of classification. Classification begins with the process of keeping universe of knowledge as a whole and dividing the same into classes and subclasses on the basis of chosen characteristic. This characteristic is normally referred to as a facet. On the whole, the classification is a progression from the general to the specific forming a hierarchical, or tree structure, each class being species of the preceding class and a genus to the following class. This process of division is akin to the biological taxonomy principle. The classes on each level, usually mutually exclusive and totally exhaustive categories, form a coordinate relationship to one another and are collocated according to the affinity of their relationships.

With a particular hierarchy, the basis for division within a class into subclasses and sub-subclasses may vary considerably from subject to subject. For example, Literature can be divided by language, genre/form or period. Architecture can be classified according to schools and styles, periods or types of buildings.

While the characteristic for division into subclass is a facet, the coordinate elements on each level or stage of division form an array. For example: Literature can be divided by language, form or period.

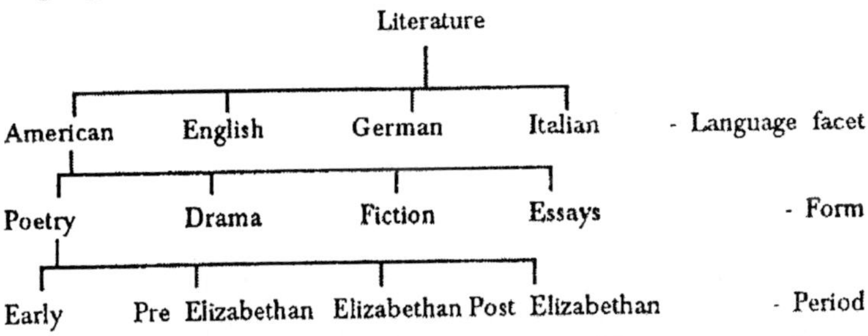

In the above example the division of Literature is based on Language facet. In Language facet coordinate elements such as American, English, German etc is an array. The term chain refers to a string of subjects, each of which represent a different level in the hierarchy. Literature - English literature - English Poetry - Elizabethan poetry.

Traditionally, Library classification schemes tend to list all the subjects and their subdivisions and provide ready made notation for them. These are called enumerative classification schemes, on the other hand, modern classification theory places emphasis on facet analysis and synthesis and hence they are called analytico-synthetic schemes. In this, the subjects are first analysed in to their component parts and then synthesised or reassembled to represent a document by notation. In an analytico synthetic scheme the intention is not to provide ready made notation but to provide more flexibility to the classifier who can analyse the subject and represent the same in the notation by a set of principles framed by the classification scheme in use. The very purpose of an analytico synthetic scheme is to identify the basic components of subjects and list under each discipline, or main class, the elements or aspects that are topically important within that class. However, in analytico synthetic schemes the facets are treated differently: one is facets that are included in a specific class and the others are common to all classes and are listed separately for application to all classes. Enumerative schemes are relatively large with long schedules as the subjects and its subdivisions and its sub subdivisions are listed exhaustively, whereas analytico synthetic schemes have small schedules without listing the subdivisions.

0.2 NOTATION

In a classification scheme, subjects are represented in the form of some symbols or letters, This is called notation of the subject. This is required to represent the subjects in brief and also their relationship. The notation is used to arrange subjects or documents in a sequential order so that the subjects can be properly designed and relationship can be easily brought out.

In some schemes, the notation consists of all letters, such a notation is termed as pure notation. The notation consisting of both letters and numbers is termed as mixed notation. Though pure notation is clear and easy to follow, the same has not been adopted by many classification schemes. The reason is simple. A pure notation can not accommodate compound and complex subjects. Hospitality in facet, array and chain can not be maintained in a pure notation. To overcome these problems, mixed notation has been employed by many a classification scheme.

Notation in a classification scheme should have characteristics of brevity, simplicity, hospitality and mnemonic. Though these characteristics are essential for a good classification scheme, they rarely co-exist in the schemes that have been brought out so far. Some of the characteristics do not supplement or complement each other, they are rather contradictory to each other. For example brevity and hospitality do not go together. If you have to accommodate all the concepts of a subject, to be classified, you would have fulfilled hospitality characteristic but not brevity characteristic. As a number formed by all concepts taken together is bound to be a long number and it defeats the purpose of the characteristic 'brevity'. The same is the case with simplicity. However, the mnemonic characteristic can be easily accommodated in a classification scheme. In fact this characteristic adds to the memory of the classificationist and classified. Mnemonic is an aid to memory. For example in Universal Decimal classification 1964 edition English literature was represented by 820 and 20 was the mnemonic for English i.e., Whenever English was to be represented in the schedule a number 20 was given, that was how earlier 420 was given for English language, and a document in English was given the language form number = 20. In Dewey Decimal Classification, Poetry is represented by the number 1, hence 811 is American Poetry, 831 is German Poetry, 841 is French Poetry and so on.

All common auxiliaries in Universal Decimal Classification can be construed as mnemonic devices only. There is another quality which notation is often expected to have, is expressiveness. This means that the notation reflects the structure or hierarchical kind as well as expressive. This quality is a valuable one because it helps the user to find his way about the systematic order. Unlike brevity, the expressiveness goes well with hospitality.

Flexibility is another important quality of notation. Knowledge is ever changing and expanding and as such notation representing that knowledge should be versatile and can not be rigid. There must be provision to accommodate new subject areas without dislocating the existing structure of the schedules. Classification schemes should select such a notation that it can be easily stretched or contracted depending on the situation that warrants. However, it is unfortunate that only a few schemes possess this quality.

0.3 CLASSIFICATION PROCESS: GENERAL GUIDELINES

As stated earlier, classification of knowledge is an art and classification process is a science. Hence classification is both art and science. Though it is not commonly understood, a classifier needs thorough knowledge in both the disciplines. i.e., Subject content of the document to be classified and classification scheme that is followed to classify the document. A person having knowledge in both these disciplines alone can provide justice to the classification of documents and the process of classification. However, a classifier can acquire thorough knowledge only by practice. He should constantly keep himself abreast of the latest developments in the universe of knowledge and correlate the knowledge with the existing scheme and accommodate the same. He should incorporate such changes and make a master copy of the classification schedule which can be termed as authority file.

If the work is on a single subject, classify it under the given subject which is a simple affair. However, a work may deal with more than one subject or more than one aspect of a subject: different subjects treated together as part of a broader subject. Interdisciplinary subjects are treated in one document and is treated as a compound subject. Such subjects require combination of class numbers from more than one schedule. But all classification schemes do not provide for such combination of classification numbers. Schemes like Universal Decimal classification, Colon classification have provision for such combination of subjects.

The following are broadly the guidelines for the classification of documents.

a. When a work can be classified under more than one subject, consider where it will be more useful to the reader and classify primarily under that subject and treat the other subjects as secondary and combine.

b. Give primary importance to the subject and then to the form or other subdivisions except in language and literature classes where form is important.

c. Use the most specific number available in the schedule. If no specific number is available, use the nearest specific number that is available. A broader number can be thought of if specificity is not required for the subject.

d. Refer to index to ascertain proximity of the subject i.e., broader subject area. Do not classify from the index alone. The number taken from the index should always be checked in the schedule to ensure that the subject of the work being classified has been placed properly in the overall structure and that the instructions in the schedules restricting or elaborating the use of the number have been observed.

e. If a compound subject is to be represented and the usefulness of both the subjects are the same to the user then classify under the first subject dealt in the book. For example: Handbook of Chemistry and Physics. Here the treatment of Chemistry and Physics are in the same proportion. Then first number in a compound number should be of Chemistry and second is Physics.

f. Phase relations like influence phase, bias phase, comparison phase, difference phase and tool phase should be represented as and when the situation warrants.

Influence phase: In a work containing two subjects: One is influenced by the other then the subject influencing should be given preference and the subject being influenced should be secondary. Religion influenced by Theology: Here Theology should have precedence over Religion.

Bias phase: A work which is written with bias towards another subject. Classify under the main subject and the subject being biased should be treated secondary subject. The work is aimed at a particular class of readers.

For example: Mathematics for Engineers. Here Mathematics will be represented first and engineers next.

Comparison phase: Classify this work under the subject emphasised or under the first subject and the subject with which it is compared gets secondary numbers.

Tool or Application phase: Classify the work under the subject to which a tool (subject) is applied. Just like bias, influence and other phases, the tool phase is a relation only. For example 'Chemical calculations: an introduction to the use of Mathematics in Chemistry' is to be classified under Chemistry with Mathematics as supplementary subject in a compound subject: Chemistry & Mathematics.

The above phase relations are only illustrative and not exhaustive. The classifier should take guidelines from these phase relations and decide on the situation, the relation that is required. These are the common phase relations that are identified by almost all classification schemes and a provision is made to represent the phase relations in the classification schemes.

0.4 COMMON DIVISIONS

In addition to the individual subjects and their subdivisions, it is necessary to represent some of the special features of a document. These features include form of a document, scope of a document, language of a document, points of view of a subject in which the document is written, geographical areas, chronological periods etc. These features have been identified as common divisions in the classification schemes. There are other common divisions which are called special common divisions that are common to a particular subject and hence listed under that subject. They are not identified by separate subject class by themselves.

Importance of common divisions is recognised by each and every classification scheme and the common divisions are isolated and separately scheduled in classification schemes as they are common to all subjects and their subdivisions. Common divisions are called by different names in different classification schemes. For example, common divisions are termed as common isolates in Colon Classification, common auxiliaries and special common auxiliaries in Universal Decimal classification and common subdivisions in Dewey Decimal classification. Though they are named differently in different classification schemes, the purpose of such common divisions is the same in all classification schemes i.e., to isolate the common concepts and represent them in the over all frame work of a classification schedule. Common divisions permit the construction of compound numbers to represent compound subjects.

0.5 CITATION CRDER

In any classification scheme the back bone is the citation order. A citation order is that in which the subjects and its subdivisions are arranged for the convenience of the users to follow the classification numbers in locating books on the shelves, subjects in a bibliography, filing of classified catalogue cards and for systematic display on a public access catalogue. Such an order must be evolved to reflect the way in which the majority of users wishes to have the material arranged. Many scientists of Library science have framed citation orders but without uniformity. However, they identified an order for the common concepts as.

Thing- Kind- Part- Material- Property- Process- Space- Time

Which means that any classification number could be decided keeping these concepts in mind. The question arises as to what is the standard order for these concepts. Different schemes have given different order for these concepts. This order can be adjusted to suit individual circumstances. But in most of the classification schedules an order is inbuilt in the hierarchy of subjects. Citation order is considered in both subject indexing and subject classification. Many studies were made on this subject and it is drawing continuous attention of the classifiers as more and more new subjects are evolved.

We have so far considered general theory of classification and normative principles that govern the classification scheme generally. Let us now consider Universal Decimal Classification system in its detail.

1

Universal Decimal Classification

1.1 INTRODUCTION

The Universal Decimal Classification (UDC) is a scheme for classifying the whole universe of knowledge. UDC has a pioneering role in systematic arrangement of a collection in libraries and arrangement of items in a subject bibliography. The schedules of the UDC have been designed to represent the true subject content of the documents. The UDC, though an offshoot of the Dewey Decimal Classification, has undergone remarkable transformation since 1937, when the first English Edition was published. Latest revision of the UDC was in 1993. 1993 revision was drawn directly from the Master Reference File (MRF). MRF is a database maintained by the UDC consortium. This database was derived from the machine readable files of the first edition of BS1000M, and was then amplified and updated.

The UDC has been published under the aegis of British Standards Institution (BSI), the national standardisation body of UK. By publishing under its fold, BSI has given a status of a standard to UDC. UDC was originally derived from Dewey

Decimal Classification and managed by the organisation now known as International Federation for Information and Documentation (FID).

In 1992, all rights and responsibilities for the UDC were transferred to the UDC consortium (UDCC) whose founder members are: AENOR (Asociacion Espanola de Normalizacion & Certificacion), Spain, Bohn Stafleu. Van Loghum, Netherlands, BSI/DISC, UK, CLPCF (Centre de lecture Publique de la communaute francaise de Belgique) Belgium, FID and INFOSTA-NIPDOK (Information Science and Technology Association) Japan.

Universal Decimal Classification published under British Standard No.1000, is now published under general licence from the UDCC, whose Executive Committee authorizes editions in various languages and at various levels of inclusiveness.

1.2 HISTORY OF THE UDC

The UDC is an offshoot of Dewey Decimal Classification so far as the principles of decimal notation is concerned. Also main classes of the UDC are based on Dewey Classes. However, the structure and characteristics of the UDC are basically different from Dewey scheme. While the Dewey scheme is totally enumerative, the UDC is an enumerative and synthetic scheme. By virtue of its synthetic nature, UDC is found favour with machine oriented retrieval systems for subject indexing. Any compound and complex subjects can be represented by the UDC notation easily.

Melvil Dewey was the first American Librarian establishing the norm of a systematic code denoting the subject as a prime means of arranging and retrieving literature in libraries - Classification of subjects. irrespective of marks identifying individual documents. He had introduced the classification scheme in 1876 and published the first edition of Dewey Decimal Classification. He used this scheme in the library of Amherst College, Massachusetts. Initially there was no decimal fraction in the scheme and hence it was not called decimal classification. Later, the three digit minimum and the decimal point after the third digit were introduced. It was expanded and its use spread rapidly throughout the USA and then in other English speaking countries.

In 1885 Paul Otlet and Henry La Fontaine were working on a project "Universal Bibligraphic Repertory" which was intended to become a comprehensive index to all published information. They were in need of a means of arranging entries in this repertory. They came across Dewey Decimal Classification then in fifth edition (1894) and were thoroughly impressed by the scheme. They found in the scheme an international language represented by numbers. They also found that because of decimal numbers, it could readily accommodate the details needed for bibliographic rather than strictly for library use. Though initially they thought of translating Dewey's scheme into French language, they decided to introduce innovation in the classification scheme by adapting purely enumerative classification into one which allows for synthesis. They also realised the concepts common to many subjects could be isolated and assembled in a separate list. These lists are tabled under auxiliary apparatus and the user can add to the main subjects wherever it is needed. As a result of this innovation, a scheme of classification which is both more copious and more sophisticated than its original was evolved. It was published under the aegis of Institute International de Bibliographie (IIB) in French from 1904 to 1907. That's how the first edition of Universal Decimal Classification took its birth under the name "Handbook to the Universal Bibliographic Repertory".

It was the turn of many scientists who shared the responsibility of expanding and revising the sections of this classification scheme. Frits Donker Duyvis of the Dutch patent office was responsible for the extensive expansion of the science and technology sections. Containing 70000 subdivisions second French edition was published during the years 1927-33 under the title "Classification Decimale Universalle". Based on this second edition, three full international editions were planned. A third edition, the first in German, published from 1934 to 1951. A fourth edition, the first in English was published in 1936-1939. Parts of this edition were published jointly by the British Society for International Bibliography and the Association of Special Libraries and Information Bureaux. (ASLIB) now Aslib, the society for Information Management. BSI assumed responsibility for publishing UDC and issued continuous English editions: Latest being International Medium edition 1993.

In 1937, Institut International de Documentation (IID) headquarters at The Hague, changed to the International Federation of Information and Documentation (FID) and remains as it is till now. FID plays a prominent role in managing and maintaining the UDC. In 1991, acting on the recommendations of the specially formed Task force for UDC System Development, it held talks with several UDC publishers about restructuring the finance, management and maintenance of the scheme and to ensure its future into the next century. As a result of these talks, the UDC consortium (UDCC) was formed, with FID, BSI and four other publishers as founder members. All the rights were transferred to the UDCC in 1992. Its first priority was the creation of a database of 60000 entries known as Master Reference File (MRF) and is now the authoritative statement of the content of the UDC. The Master Reference File is currently in English, but it will be extended to include French and German and other languages later. The UDC has been translated to many other languages and there are editions in 23 different languages.

The UDC differs from other schemes so far as the revision of classification schedules is concerned. This has a continuous revision policy since its inception in 1904. This means that new subjects are included whenever such an inclusion is warranted. Missing concepts previously overlooked can be considered immediately without waiting till a new edition is published. Such changes are brought out in the form of 'Extensions and Corrections to the UDC' which is a loose leaf updating service. Users can take advantage of this updating service for their classification practice. Users can also suggest to the UDCC for any proposals to improve the UDC for the inclusion of missing concepts and new subjects that crop up from time to time.

1.3 STRUCTURE

UDC is a mixture of two kinds of documentary classification schemes. It has both enumerative and analytico synthetic characters. While schedules in the main table of the UDC can be termed as enumerative, the auxiliary tables exemplify analytico synthetic character. The notation is almost pure with Arabic numerals having their own inherent ordinal value. Except for alphabetic devices, no alphabet is used in the notation. Because of numerals, the base of UDC is very large to accommodate new subjects in its fold without disturbing the existing subjects. This concept fulfills the characteristic of a notation: hospitality in array.

1.3.1 Main tables.

In the UDC, universe of knowledge is taken as a unity (1) and subdivided into 10 divisions. The notation and division of universe of knowledge into 10 divisions is similar to the Dewey's scheme. Each of the 10 divisions are further subdivided. The 10 divisions are numbered 0-9 except 4, which class is presently vacant. Originally class 4 was allotted Linguistics and now Linguistics is grouped under class 8 by leaving class 4 blank. The main classes in the UDC are

0. Generalities Science and knowledge. Organization. Information etc.
1. Philosophy. Psychology.
2. Religion. Theology.
3. Social Sciences. Law. Government etc.
4. Vacant.
5. Mathematics and Natural Sciences.
6. Applied Sciences. Medicine. Technology.
7. The arts. Recreation. Entertainment. Sport.

8. Language. Linguistics. Literature.
9. Geography. Biography. History.

Each of these classes are denoted by three digit number in Dewey Decimal classification. Because of single digit in UDC, each class can accommodate more number of concepts. For example class 5 can be divided into ten subclasses.

50. Generalities about the Pure Sciences
51. Mathematics.
52. Astronomy. Astrophysics. Space Research. Geodesy.
53. Physics.
54. Chemistry. Crystallography. Mineralogical Sciences.
55. Earth Sciences. Geology. Meteorology etc.
56. Paleontology.
57. Biological Sciences in general.
58. Botany.
59. Zoology.

One digit class is divided into two digit subclass with a prefix of the main class from which it is derived. Now two digit subclass is divided into three digit subdivision and the division continues as long as the depth of the subject is to be represented. Thus the main classes are divided hierarchically, with the numeric hierarchy reflecting the conceptual hierarchy, the broadest classes are at the highest level and the narrowest or most restrictive classes are at the lowest level of the hierarchy. As the subdivision of each class goes on to the extent of representing depth classification, the length of the class number is indicative of the degree of detail.

The ordinal value of a number depends on its being regarded as decimal fraction, less than unity. For the convenience, all main classes are represented by a single digit. As a visual aid, a decimal point is introduced after every three digits. They do not have the same order as integers hence they are pronounced as a series of digits like six, two, one point three instead of six hundred twenty one point three.

The division of main class 6 is as follows:

6. Applied Sciences. Medicine. Technology.
60. General Matters.
61. Medical Sciences.
62. Engineering. Technology in general.
63. Agriculture and related sciences and techniques.
64. Housekeeping. Home economics.
65. Management and Organization of industry, trade, communication.
66. Chemical technology. Chemical and related industries.
67. Various industries, trades and crafts.
68. Finished or assembled articles. Precision Mechanism.
69. Building trade. Materials. Practices etc.

Again each of these subclasses are further divided to represent the subjects in depth. Subclass 62 is divided further as follows.

621. Mechanical Engineering. Nuclear Technology. Electrical Engineering.
622. Mining.
623. Military Engineering.
624. Civil and Structural Engineering in general.
625. Railway Engineering. Highway Engineering.
626. General Hydraulic Engineering. Canal Engineering.
627. Natural Waterway, Port and Shore Engineering. Communication.
628. Public Health Engineering. Water. Sanitation. Illuminating engineering.
629. Transport Vehicle Engineering.

Further subdivision of 621 into 10 divisions:

621.0 Mechanical Engineering theory, Nuclear Technology.

621.1 Heat engines in general. Generation, distribution and use of steam.

621.2 Hydraulic energy, water power. Hydraulic machinery.

621.3 Electrical Engineering.

621.4 Heat Engines. Internal Combustion Engines. etc.,

621.5 Pneumatic energy. Refrigeration. Liquefaction.

621.6 Fluids handling, Storage and distribution. Pumps, Pipes etc.,

621.7 Plastic or Chipless working, forming and treatment of materials.

621.8 Mechanical power transmission. Gearing. Materials handling. Fasteners. Lubrication.

621.9 Working or machining with chip formation. Machine tools.

Each of these divisions again subdivided into 10 subclasses.

The total divisions and subdivisions are represented in schematic thus:

UDC SCHEMATIC

UDC Scheme is given on next page.

1.3.2 Auxiliary tables

UDC's most innovative and influential feature was its auxiliary notation which provides for constructing compound number or a synthetic number. A classification number taken from only a single class from main tables or from an independent auxiliary is a simple number. Numbers 531, 621.3 etc. are some of the examples., A number coined by taking independent numbers from more than one place in the main tables or in the auxiliary table is a compound number. Compound numbers are required to represent the complete thought content of a document so that the contents of the documents can be accessed from different approaches. The necessity of such a representation is growing because of

The Universe of Information

- 0 Generalities. Science and knowledge. Organization. Information etc.
- 1. Philosophy. Psychology
- 2. Religion Theology
- 3. Social sciences. Law. Government
- 4. (Vacant)
- 5. Mathematics and natural sciences
- 6. Applied sciences. Medicine. Technology
    - 60 General matters
    - 61 Medical sciences
    - 62 Engineering. Technology in general
        - 620 Materials testing. Commercial materials etc.
        - 621 Mechanical engineering. Nuclear technology. Electrical engineering
        - 622 Mining
        - 623 Military engineering
        - 624 Civil and structural engineering in general
        - 625 Railway engineering. Highway engineering
        - 626 General hydraulic engineering. Canal engineering etc.
        - 627 Natural waterway, port and shore engineering
        - 628 Public health engineering. Water. Sanitation. Illuminating engineering
        - 629 Transport vehicle engineering
    - 63 Agriculture and related sciences and techniques
    - 64 Housekeeping. Home economics
    - 65 Management and organization of industry, trade, communication
    - 66 Chemical technology. Chemical and related industries
    - 67 Various industries, trades and crafts
    - 68 Finished or assembled articles Precision mechanisms
    - 69 Building trade. Materials. Practice etc.
- 7. Arts. Recreation. Entertainment. Sport
- 8. Languages Linguistics. Literature
- 9. Geography. Biography. History

Contd.........

621.0
Mechanical engineering theory. Nuclear technology

621.1
Heat engines in general. Generation, distribution and use of steam

621.2
Hydraulic energy. Water power. Hydraulic machinery

621.3
Electrical engineering

621.4
Heat engines (except steam engines). Internal combustion engines etc.

621.5
Pneumatic energy. Refrigeration. Liquefaction

621.6
Fluids handling, storage and distribution. Pumps, pipes etc.

621.7
Plastic or chipless working, forming and treatment of materials

621.8
Mechanical power transmission. Gearing. Materials handling. Fasteners. Lubrication

621.9
Working or machining with chip formation. Machine tools

621.31
Generation, supply and control of electricity. Measurement

621.32
Electric lamps

621.33
Electric traction, locomotion, propulsion

621.35
Electrochemical technology

621.36
Thermoelectricity. Electric heating

621.37
Technique of electric waves, electromagnetic waves, oscillations, pulses

621.38
Electronic devices. Electron tubes. Photocells. Particle accelerators. X-ray tubes

621.39
Telecommunication. Telecontrol. Radio, television etc.

621.391
General communication questions. Cybernetics, information theory etc.

621.394
Telegraphy

621.395
Telephony

621.396
Radio communication. Sound transmission etc.

621.397
Picture transmission. Television

621.398
Telecontrol. Telemetering. Remote indication

621.396.1
Generalities. Early experiments etc.

621.396.2
Transmission systems, type of wave

621.396.4
Multiple transmission. Directional transmission

621.396.6
Radio conununication apparatus and circuits. Transmitters. Receivers

621.396.7
Radio stations. Transmitting and receiving stations

621.396.9
Special radio apparatus and methods. Radar

Courtesy : UDC *International Medium Edition, 1993*

interdisciplinary nature of subjects in the present day of technological developments.

As mentioned earlier, the importance of isolating certain common concepts was realised by many classification schemes. Hence they provided a separate class or a list of tables for such concepts. These tables serve as a linkage for one class to another class thereby achieving flexibility in the classification scheme. It is felt that such a flexibility is required because of interdisciplinary nature of subjects. Common divisions, Common isolates, auxiliary divisions are some of the tables fall in this category in some of the classification schemes.

Most of the tables listing these common aspects are enumerative and synthetic. Auxiliary notation is of two types: the common and special auxiliaries. The common auxiliaries not only provide a means of expressing interrelations between subjects, but also denote generally recurrent characteristics that are applicable throughout the schedule(main tables). The special auxiliaries denote locally recurrent characteristics i.e., those that are applicable in a limited range of the main tables.

The common auxiliaries are again in two types of symbols: Signs and subdivisions.

Signs: +(Plus), /(Stroke), :(Colon), [ ](Square brackets), ::(Double colon).

Subdivisions: Numeric tables representing Space and Time, Language names, Forms, Nationality, Persons and Personal Characteristics.

The common auxiliary subdivisions fall into two groups: The independent and the dependent auxiliary tables. The numbers from the independent auxiliary table, though may be affixed to any UDC number where appropriate, may also be used on their own, to form the whole class number for a document. Tables of Form, Language, Place, Nationality and Time are examples of independent auxiliary tables. For example, a dictionary or an encyclopedia (form of document) can be represented by a number taken from Form table alone. Likewise the Space (Place) can be represented by taking a number from Space table, whereas a dependent auxiliary tables must be, as their very name indicates, affixed to main table numbers. Tables of Points of view, Materials, Persons are examples of dependent auxiliary tables. Numbers taken from Points of view table are to be attached to the main UDC numbers with a point(.) and numbers taken from Materials and Persons are to be attached to the main UDC numbers with a hyphen(-). Hyphen sign should not be mistaken for a similar sign in 62 Main class schedule where -1/-9 are the special auxiliary subdivisions. What we consider here are common auxiliary subdivisions and that too dependent auxiliary subdivisions.

Independent auxiliary subdivisions have also symbols but the need to attach them to the main class is flexible. They can be prefixed, suffixed and infixed (putting in between two numbers). These symbols have biterminal signs i.e., they will have opening and closing element. This has been done in order to demarcate the auxiliary numbers from the adjacent main numbers. Form numbers have parentheses, while Nationality and Time have quotation marks as connecting symbols. However, Language number has =(equal to) connecting symbol which has only an initial equals sign. This symbol though exception from biterminal sign, has a colon at the end to compensate the biterminal sign. The following examples should make things more clear.

Independent auxiliaries:

Encyclopedia 031

Encyclopedia of Chemistry 54(031)

Map - Great Britain 084.31(420)

Climatological maps 551.582(084.31)

As explained earlier, the independent auxiliaries can exist on their own without depending on the main UDC numbers.

Dependent auxiliaries:

Power Plant

reliability 621.311.2.004.15

Machinery details 62-1/-9

Medical Staff: Doctors.
Nurses 616-051
Metal fibre technology 669-037.53
Criticism of Russian
literature 821.161.1.09
Copper Zinc alloys 669.35'5'6

As mentioned earlier, the dependent auxiliaries .00, -,' have to be used with the help of main UDC numbers. In the above examples, Power Plant reliability 621.311.2.004.15, .004.15 is taken from the points of view table, Machinery details 62-1/-9, -1/-9 are special auxiliaries listed under 62 Engineering class and must be used only for that class. Medical Staff 616-051,-051 is taken from the Common auxiliaries of Persons and personal characteristics. Metal fibre technology 669-037.53, -037.53 is taken from -03 common auxiliaries of materials. 821.161.1.09 Criticism of Russian Literature, .01/.09 are also special auxiliaries and must be used only wherever they are listed. Though there is similarity between -1/-9 and .01/.09, .01/.09 provide subsets of recurrent concepts such as plant operation, processes and equipment. In this example the subdivisions .01/.09 are listed under theory, studies and techniques of literature. 82.09 is literary criticism. 821.161.1 is Russian literature. Since this is a dependent auxiliary .09 can be attached to the main class 82 and its subdivisions. In the example Copper Zinc Tin alloys 669.35'5'6. Here 669.35 is Copper, 669.5 is Zinc alloys and 669.6 Tin alloys. The apostrophe is specially used under instructions at alloys in 669...5 Metallurgy class. They are often synthetic and integrative in function, denoting compound subjects by compound notation. They are some times fully listed but elsewhere are derived from main numbers by parallel subdivision.

Special auxiliaries may be used either singly or in combination with other auxiliaries. They appear with other auxiliary tables as well as in the main tables.

PARALLEL DIVISION ≡

This is another device similar to special auxiliary device. It is indicated in the tables by the subdivide as sign ≡. This means that the number preceding ≡ may be subdivided in a manner analogous to the number following it. For expressing the same concept in different classes this device is used. For example in Medicine 61 class, the subdivisions in 611 and 616 are parallel and hence can be represented with the same digits in both the places. Under 611.3 Apparatus Digestorius. Digestive system. Alimentary canal, it is given as 611.3 ≡ 616.3. Here the concept is Digestive system. It appears both in Anatomy and Pathology. Hence the divisions of Digestive system are common in both the places instead of repeating the divisions under 611.3 and 616.3 classes, it is divided under 616.3 and the same is to be applied at 611.3 as per the instructions. This means that all subdivisions listed under 616.3 are attached to 611.3 without any connecting symbol to represent anatomy aspect of that concept. Suppose we have to represent anatomy of throat: the number looks like 611.321 whereas pathology of throat is 616.321. Likewise we have 611.833 Cervical Nerves (611.831/.835 ≡ 616.833.1/.5). Anatomy of Auditory Nerve will have a number 611.831.8. Pathology of auditory Nerve has a number 616.833.18. Since 611.831/.835 is to be subdivided analogous to 616.833.1/.5 anatomy of auditory Nerve will have the above number 611.831.8. (611.831 = 616.833.1). Hence 616.833.18 will be applicable as 611.831.8. We will find a number of instances of these parallel divisions in the schedules.

There is no limit to the kinds of notation where parallel division is used. They may be main numbers, they may be auxiliary divisions, special auxiliaries, common auxiliaries etc. It can be in the same class itself (659.28 ≡ 659.2). This device is one of the many mnemonic devices that the UDC has used. This serves dual purpose one is digit saving and avoiding separate subdivision process and the other as mnemonic device.

RELATION SIGN : (COLON)

Colon is used to represent relations between one subject

and another subject. This relation sign is quite common as many compound subjects are to be represented in interdisciplinary subjects and interdisciplinary subdivisions. The relation sign extends the scope of subjects contained in a document. It also helps to represent the subjects in their proper perspective. Colon sign is extensively used in Colon Classification to represent relations among subjects. Phase relations are represented separately in Colon Classification. But in UDC only colon is used for all the relations irrespective of their nature. We have seen that five types of phase relations are identified in the classification schemes. a) General b) Bias c) Influence d) Difference and e) Comparison. While colon classification has separate devices for these five phase relations, UDC has only colon device for all these relations. eg.

Ethics in relation to art	17:7
Mathematics for Engineers	51:62
Computers in Chemistry	54:681.3
Difference between Physics and Chemistry	53:54
Influence of the bible on English literature	22:820
Applications of Data processing to industrial Management.	658:681.3

These relations can be represented by reversing the order like A:B or B:A depending on the individual library where the subjects of specialisation is of paramount importance. For example in the case of 'Application of data Processing in industrial management 658:681.3' in the libraries where management subject is important the number can be 658:681.3, alternately where Data processing is the core subject of the library the number can be 681.3:658.

However, there is another device where these relations can not be altered, that is order fixing device represented by :: (Double colon). With this notation the number after double colon is a subordinate concept of the preceding number and the whole number is treated by the system as unity and not two separate identities as is the case with colon (:) illustrated in the following example

International Federation for Documentation (FID)

061.2(100) :: 002 FID

Here the order of subjects are Union, International, Documentation, by name FID.

In this case the entry in the classified portion is only by 061.2 and no entry under 002 as it does not form an independent class so far as this title is concerned.

This double colon differs with single colon in which an entry is made for the numbers succeeding colon and hence the numbers can be reversed.

SUB GROUPING: [ ] (SQUARE BRACKETS)

This symbol was first introduced in 1985. This is used as a subgrouping within a complex combination of UDC numbers in order to classify the relationship of the components. It is needed when a subject denoted by two or more UDC numbers linked by a plus sign, stroke or colon is as a whole related to another number by colon.

For example: Handbook of Chemistry and Physics.

[54+53](035)

Solar energy Materials

[620.91:523.72]:620.1

Education in Indo British schools.

37:[540+420]

Flow induced vibrations in turbomachinery.

[532.5:534.01]:621-15

1.4 CITATION ORDER

UDC with its enumerative principle, has provided many devices, symbols and auxiliaries. Having come across so many provisions it is a bit puzzling to arrange these numbers and devices to form an integrated notation. Hence there is a need to know as to how these can be sequenced.

In a notation where facets are represented in a particular order the arrangement is called facet formula. This is also denoted as citation order.

In UDC the citation order is elements in a compound class number proceed from special to general. UDC has followed the principle of inversion in fixing the citation order for its class numbers. It means that the order of elements in a classification number is exactly reverse to the order of the auxiliaries listed in UDC schedules. The order of schedules for various auxiliaries is:

= Language
(0...) form
(1/9) space
(=...) Nationality
"..." Time
+ Extension
/ Extension
Simple number
: Relation
:: Order fixing
.00 Points of view
-0
-1/-9
.0
.1/.9
,

In a citation order this is exactly in the reverse order. The schedules are so arranged that the principle of general view to specific view is followed. In a citation order, therefore, the principle of specific view to general view is followed. This is required when we have to classify a document containing many facets.

For example:Indian Industries Directory.

Here three facets: Space, Subject, Form are to be represented.

Space : (540) India

Subject : 6 Industry

Form : (058) Directory

As per the above citation order, the notation for this title should be 6(540) (058)

Mathematical tables in Russian.

Subject : Mathematics : 51

Form : Tables : (083.5)

Language : Russian : =161.1

The notation is 51(083.5)=161.1

Twentieth Century Physics : a pictorial book in German.

Subject : Physics : 53

Period : 20th century :"19"

Form : Pictorial book : (084)

Language : German : = 133.1

The notation would be 53"19"(084) = 133.1

In the schedule, Language tables are listed prior to Form table followed by Time. Hence in the notation the arrangement is Time followed by Form and Language.

The citation order for various auxiliaries and their subdivisions in UDC is:

Main Number,	Special auxiliaries,	Common auxiliaries
0/9	.01/.09 and -0/-9	Points of view .00

Time " ", Place (1/9), Form (0), Language =

1.5 FILING ORDER

After classifying the document, the question of filing order comes into picture. In any classification system the normal filing order is based on the principle of progression from the general to the particular. Thus the common auxiliaries which are used as independent auxiliaries are filed before a main class number since the common auxiliaries are treated as general numbers. Next, a compound number with + and / as connecting symbols are filed as the subjects represented by these symbols are of general nature without being specific. The compound number is followed by a simple main class number and this main class number in turn is followed by a number with a common auxiliary or special auxiliary as the number with a common auxiliary is more specific than a simple number(without common auxiliary). The numbers will follow the order of strict hierarchic division with each successive division further sharpening the concept thereby increasing its particularity.

The symbols in table 1a, the + and / (Plus and Stroke) extend rather than restrict the meaning of a number and compound number with these symbols files before the simple number itself. Filing order is given schematic as:

INDEPENDENT AUXILIARIES

Symbol	*Example*
Addition +	53+55 Physics and Geology
Extension /	5/6 Science and Technology.
Simple Number	621.3 Electrical Engineering

AUXILIARIES AS SUFFIXES

Relation (reversible)	:	681.3:63 Computers in Agriculture (this can also be reversed to form 63:681.3)
Relation (Non reversible)	::	658::681.3 Management services influenced by Computers
Language	=	621.313 = 112.2 Electrical machines in German
Form	(0..)	621.01(035) Mechanical Engineering Handbook
Place	(1/9)	621.01(540) Developments in Mechanical Engineering in India.
Nationality	(=)	621.01-051(=1.540)Mechanical Engineers Indian Nationals.
Time	" "	63"19" Agriculture in 20th century
Alphabetical device	A/Z	681.3.06COBOL Computer Programming COBOL

Points of view	.00	621.01.004.15 Reliability in Mechanical Engineering
Persons	-0	621.01-051 Chartered Mechanical Engineers.

SPECIAL AUXILIARIES

-1/-9	621.01-78 Safety devices in Mechanical Engineering.
.0	677.05 Textile Machinery and equipment.
'0/'9	547.29'26 Acid alcohol esters

Next Simple Number comes in continuation to the above numbers as the case may be. In case of 621.01, the next simple number is 621.1, for 677.05 it is 677.1 and for 681.3.06 it is 681.31.

The filing order is required both in card catalogue and shelf arrangement in a library. In case of bibliographies and subject indexes also the filing order is very important.

1.6 CLASSIFIED INDEX

It is customary that each library provides at least two sequences (author, editor, compiler, corporate author etc) and classified sequence (By classification number). It has been proved time and again that these sequences generally satisfy the approaches made by the user to the card catalogue in a special library.

In a classified sequence, UDC numbers, especially compound numbers pose ticklish problems. The very purpose of providing a compound number, to classify the book in depth, is defeated if the classified file contains entry at one point only. There will not be an approach by other numbers to the classified sequence. For example a book with title 'Handbook of Chemistry and Physics' is classified as 54+53(035). If it were to be filed under only one sequence, this card would have been filed under 54 sequence and there would not have been entries for the other facets 53 and (035) and as such no approach through these facets would have been possible. In natural language, this book Handbook of Chemistry and Physics, would be traced only through Chemistry subject approach. There will not be approaches to the subject Physics and form 'handbook' which is not correct. The subjects concerned with the book like Physics and handbook would be missing for the users of these subjects.

To overcome this difficulty, It is advisable to prepare different approaches to the class number. In this case multiple entries are made under Physics 53 and handbook (035) in addition to Chemistry 54 as main entry. Three classified catalogue cards are prepared for the three facets. 54, 53 and (035) and each is filed under its respective sequence. However all the three cards will have only one number in that order as 54+53(035). The card filed under 54 is main card and the card filed under 53 will have 53 underlined like 54+53(035) and card filed under (035) will have (035) underlined i.e. 54+53 *(035)*. Accordingly the three cards are filed under their respective sequences i.e 54+53 (035) under 54 Chemistry, 54+53(035) under 53 Physics and 54+53*(035)* under (035) handbooks. This kind of arrangement in classified files helps not only for multivarious subjects approach but also to know the number of various document forms like handbooks, dictionaries, encyclopedias etc that are available in the library through the classified file. Though the actual arrangement of these forms on the shelves is scattered, the card catalogue brings all of them at one place by virtue of their numbers. Also, the cards are scattered in classified sequence by virtue of their approaches, Whereas the book is kept under main number sequence i.e. 54+53 (035) under Chemistry section. In a machine readable catalogue file the above arrangement is not required as the software will take care of different approach points to the data base.

1.7 SUMMARY OF THE CLASSIFICATION SCHEDULES

The following are the broad outlines of subjects in UDC schedule. UDC has isolated the common features of various concepts that are recurrent in various subjects. Separate schedules(tables) are provided for each of the common auxiliaries mentioned below. Instead of repeating these common auxiliaries in every main class, UDC has scheduled them under one common table. These tables have to be consulted every time whenever any concept needs to be represented from the concerned table.

COMMON AUXILIARIES: SIGNS

+ Coordination

/ Extension

: Relations

[ ] Sub grouping

:: Order fixing

* Non UDC notation

A/Z Alphabetical device.

-1/-9,.01/.09,'0/'9 Special auxiliary subdivisions

COMMON AUXILIARIES: TABLES

= Language

(0..) Form

(1/9) Place

(=..) Nationality

" " Time

.00 Points of View

-3 Materials

-5 Persons and personal characteristics

For all the above common auxiliaries schedules of tables are provided. Common auxiliaries of Language under table 1c are listed from page No.2 of the schedule and continues upto page No.15 (14 pages are allotted). Common auxiliaries of Form under table 1d are listed from page No.15 and continued upto page No.20 (6 Pages). Common auxiliaries of Place under table 1e are listed from page No.21 to page No.65(45 pages). Table 1f is for common auxiliaries of Nationality. It starts on page

No.65 and ends on page No.66 (only 2 pages). Table 1g is for common auxiliaries of Time listed from page No.66 to page No.72. Then comes common auxiliaries of Points of View. Table 1i starts on page No.73 and ends on page No.76. Last table before the start of Main classes is the table 1k: Common auxiliaries of general characteristics. A table for both materials and persons. This table has occupied pages from 76 to 82 (7 pages). Altogether there are 83 pages for auxiliary tables in the UDC 1993 International Medium edition Pt 1. Systematic tables.

After the listing of tables for common auxiliaries the main tables are listed. The main tables are also called as schedules of classification. The main tables are thus called because the classes they represent are main classes from which many subclasses are branched out. Also the subject concepts can be represented independently with the help of these main classes. whereas the schedules of auxiliary tables are subordinate and hence can not be independently used to represent the concepts for which they are assigned. Let us list out the main tables with immediate subdivisions for illustrative purpose. This list is by no means exhaustive. The reader is advised to consult the schedules of the UDC for a full picture of main classes and their subdivisions and sub-subdivisions etc,

MAIN CLASSES

0 **Generalities, Science and Knowledge.** Organisation. Information. Documentation. Librarianship. Institutions. Publications.

00 Prolegomena. Fundamentals of Knowledge and culture.

01 Bibliography and bibliographies. Catalogues.

02 Librarianship.

03 *Vacant.*

030 Encyclopedias. General reference works.

04 *Vacant.*

05 *Vacant.*

050 Serial publications. Periodicals (journals, magazines etc).

06 Organisations and other types of cooperation. Associations. Congresses. Exhibitions. Museums.

07 *Vacant.*

070 News papers. Journalism. The press.

08 Polygraphies. Collective works.

09 Manuscripts. Rare and remarkable works.

1 Philosophy, Psychology.

11 Metaphysics.

12 *Vacant.*

13 Philosophy of mind and spirit. Metaphysics of Spiritual life.

14 Philosophical systems and points of View. Weltan schauung.

15 *Vacant.*

159.9 Psychology.

16 Logic. Epistemology. Theory of knowledge. Methodology of Logic.

17 Moral Philosophy. Ethics. Practical Philosophy.

18 *Vacant.*

19 *Vacant.*

2 Religion, Theology

21 National theology. Theodicy. De Deo. Rational theology. Religious philosophy.

22 The Bible. Holy scripture.

23/28 Christianity. The christian religion.

23 Dogmatic theology.

24 Practical theology.

25 Pastoral theology.

26 Christian church in general (nature and character).

27 General history of the Christian Church.

28 Christian Churches, Sects, denominations.

29 Non Christian religions.

3 Social Sciences, Statistics, Politics, Economics.

Trade. Law. Government. Military Affairs. Welfare. Insurance. Education. Folklore.

30 Theories, methodology and methods in the social sciences. Sociography.

31 Demography. Sociology. Statistics.

32 Politics.

33 Economics. Economic Science.

34 Law. Jurisprudence.

35 Public administration. Government. Military Affairs.

36 Ensuring the mental and material needs in life. Social work. Social aid. Housing. Insurance.

37 Education. Teaching. Training. Leisure.

38 *Vacant.*

389 Metrology. Weights and Measures.

39 Ethnology. Ethnography. Customs. Manners. Traditions. Way of Life. Folklore.

4 *Vacant.*

5 Mathematics and Natural Sciences.

50 *Vacant.*

501 Generalities about pure sciences.

502 Nature. Nature study and conservation. Nature and Wildlife protection.

503 *Vacant.*

504 Environmental Science. Environmentology.

505 –

509 *Vacant.*

51 Mathematics

52 Astronomy. Astrophysics. Space Research. Geodesy.

53 Physics.

54 Chemistry. Crystallography. Mineralogical Sciences.

55 Earth Sciences. Geology. Meteorology etc.

56 Paleontology.

57 Biological Sciences in general.

58 Botany.

59 Zoology.

6 Applied Sciences. Medicine. Technology.

60 General Questions of Applied Sciences.

61 Medicine. Medical Sciences.

62 Engineering. Technology in general.

620 Materials testing. Commercial Materials.

621 Mechanical engineering in general. Machinery. Hydraulic energy. Nuclear technology.

621.1 Mechanical Engineering.

621.3 Electrical Engineering.

621.38 Electronic Engineering.

622 Mining.

623 Military Engineering.

624 Civil Engineering.

625.1/.5 Railway Engineering.

625.7/.8 Highway Engineering.

626 Hydraulic Engineering in general.

627 Natural Waterways.

628 Public Health Engineering.

629 Transport Vehicle Engeneering.

63 Agricultural Sciences.

64 Home economics.

65 Management and Organisation of Industry, trade and Communications.

66 Chemical Technology. Chemical and related industries.

67 Various industries. Trades and Crafts.

68 Industries, Crafts and Trades for finished or assembled articles.

69 Building (construction) trade. Building materials Building practice.

7 The Arts, Recreation, Entertainment, Sport.

71 Physical planning. Regional, town and country planning. Landscapes, parks, gardens.

72 Architecture.

73 Plastic arts.

74 Drawing. Design. Applied Arts and crafts.

75 Painting.

76 Graphic arts. Graphics.

77 Photography and similar processes .

78 Music.

79 Recreation, Entertainment. Games. Sport.

8 Language, Linguistics. Literature.

80 General questions relating to both Linguistics and Literature. Philology.

81 Linguistics and Languages.

82 Literature.

89,83 *Vacant*

9 Geography, Biography, History.

902/904 Archaeology. Prehistory.

908 Area Studies. Study of a locality .

91 Geography. Exploration of the Earth and of individual countries. Travel. Regional Geography.

92 *Vacant.*

929 Biographical and related studies.

93/99 History.

990 History of Oceania, the Polar regions, Australia etc.

994 History of Australia.

2

Use of Auxiliary Tables

2.1 INDEPENDENT COMMON AUXILIARIES.

a) *Coordination*:connecting symbol +

The sign for coordination function is +. The coordination sign connects two or more non consecutive UDC numbers to denote a compound subject for which no single UDC number is enumerated in the schedule.

For example : Biology and Medicine.

Here two subjects are dealt within a book. Simple UDC numbers do exist for each of these classes separately. But there is no compound number. Hence it is necessary to coin a compound number. The two classes Biology and Medicine have classification numbers 57 and 61 respectively. As the two classes are not consecutive in the schedules, the sign + is used to combine these non consecutive numbers. The number is 57+61. The number can be reversed also. But it is functionally advisable to go by the subject coverage in the book i.e the major subject gets precedence over the minor subject. Then naturally the title would also go by the sequence of major and minor subjects covered in the book. In case of a book with title

Medicine and Biology it is obvious that Medicine is majority subject and accordingly the class number for the book is 61+57. For providing approach to both the subjects in a classified catalogue, it is advisable to provide additional cards under 61 and 57.

Some more examples for the use of coordination sign.

CRC Hand Book of Chemistry and Physics : 54+53(035)

Text book of calculus and analytical geometry : 517.2 + 514.13

Mining and Metallurgy : 622+669

It is to be noted that the coordination sign is used only when there is no phase relation among the subjects. However, when phase relation is to be used it should be represented by :. More under the relation sign heading.

b) *Extension*: connecting symbol /

Extension of subjects is represented by using the connecting symbol / (stroke). While the coordination sign + is used to combine two non consecutive class numbers, the extension / is used to combine two consecutive numbers. The sign can be used both in main classes and in auxiliaries also. A series of classes in a row can be represented with the help of extension sign.

For example : Theory of machines is given a number 62-1/-9

Here the consecutive numbers -1 to -9 details are covered. Hence the / (stroke) is used to connect the numbers. This is within the same class 62. Between two main classes the number would be like 641/642 Food and Meals. Main class 641 is for Food cooking and Main Class 642 is for Meals and Meal times. In the case of Systematic Zoology 592/599 classes of 592, 593, 594... 599 are all covered in this title. While the stroke sign is the same in all classes be it a main class or a subclass, in a main class a distinction is made between the main classes and subclasses while using the stroke sign.

For example the title 'Theory of electricity and magnetism' will have a notation as 537.1/.6. Here 537 is a main class and 537.1 Electricity theory and 537.6 Magnetism theory are subclasses. There exists a relation between these two subclasses so far as the title Theory of electricity and magnetism is concerned. To represent the relation among subclasses the notation 537.1/537.6 is generally to be assigned. But instead of giving a notation like this, the notation 537.1/.6 is given since these two are the subclasses of the same main class. This saves the number of digits and the length of the notation . However, while filing the cards for this compound subject 537.1/.6 two cards are prepared as usual. But the second card (first card is filed under 537.1) is filed under 537.6 though the whole number is not mentioned as such on the card.

c) *Simple relation*: symbol :

The relation sign : (colon) indicates a relationship between two or more subjects by connecting their UDC numbers. For any phase relation the colon sign is used in the UDC . The relation is reversible and general. The classes thus connected with : are of equal significance howsoever they are positioned i.e. before or after the :

For example, the title "Engineering management" will have a notation 62:65. In this case the stress is more on engineering and therefore, the book is given first notation as 62. To stress the point that this can be a reversible relation, 65:62 also can be made to represent a book 'Management techniques in Engineering'.

Colon symbol is used extensively in UDC system. Examples using colon symbol.

Biophysics 57:53	
Engineering thermodynamics	62:536.7
Analysis of polymers	541.64:543
Electronic measurement and instrumentation	621.38:621.317

Illustrations

1) Administrative Law of cultural affairs 342.951:351.85

34 Law

342 Public Law. Administrative Law

342.9 Administrative Law

342.95 Specialised Administrative Law

342.951 Administrative Law of subject areas

35 Public Administration. Government. Military Affairs.

351 Particular Activities of Administration

351.85 Cultural Administration.

2) Loading and Unloading devices on freight vehicles.

621.869:629.114.4

621 Mechanical Engineering

621.8 Power Transmission.

621.86 Materials Handling

621.869 Loading and Unloading devices

629 Transport Vehicle Engineering

629.1 Land Vehicles and water craft engineering

629.11 Land Vehicles Engineering Road vehicles

629.114 Motor Vehicles according to purpose

629.114.4 Freight (goods) Vehicles.

The above illustrations show how intrinsically the UDC numbers can be derived with the help of colon :. Practically there is no limitation for using colon sign. There can be more than one colon sign in a classification number. For example 'Solar energy materials' is given a notation 620.91:523.72:620.1. Here Solar Energy is a compound subject derived by combining the subjects sun and energy and the compound subject is related to material aspect. Once again a compound subject. The number is analysed as

620.9 Economics of energy

620.91 Energy resources. Natural resources

52 Astronomy

523 Solar System

523.72 Sun

620.1 Materials Testing. Commercial materials. Protection of materials.

There is ample provision in the UDC for giving enough representation to all the concepts of a subject or subjects. The only drawback with UDC numbers is their unusual length and so the problems in their usage on spines of books and on catalogue cards.

d) *Subgrouping* : Symbol [ ]

This symbol was first introduced in 1985 edition. The usage is not much in practice.

Square brackets may be used as a subgrouping like in algebra when two or more numbers are linked by a connecting symbol to denote a complex subject which is again related to another by colon or any auxiliary division.

For example:

Mining and Metallurgy in USSR [622+669] (57)

Computers in biophysics 681.3 : [57:53]

More visuals are added to the number by introducing [ ] sign. The monotonous nature of the classification number can be broken by introducing a sign like this. The number will otherwise look like 681.3:57:53.

e) *Order - fixing* sign ::

The double colon may be used to fix the order of the component numbers in a compound number, especially for machine readable data. Whenever a subordinate relationship is to be indicated to the preceding concept, this sign is used in between these two relationships. When this sign is used, the whole number is taken as a unity and there are no two simple numbers but only compound number.

For example:

Cytogenetics 575::576.3.

Here for all practical purposes 575 class only is taken into account. The relation can not be reversed unlike in :. That's how 576.3 has no independent status for filing or retrieval so far as this compound number is concerned.

Illustration:

International Federation for Documentation FID. 061.2(100):: 002 FID

Here the order of subjects are union, international, documentation, name FID

06 Organisation and other types of cooperation

061 Societies. Associations. Congresses.

061.2 Private Organisations. Societies. Associations.

(100) Universe - Place table.

002 Documentation

FID Alphabetical device.

This auxiliary has only a limited use when used in a manual system.

f) *Common auxiliaries of Language*: Symbol =

The common auxiliaries of Language denote the Language or Linguistic form of a document whose subject is denoted by a main UDC number. The subjects are derived for class 8 from the schedules of Language. The table of common auxiliaries of Language acts as a mnemonic device for the Language and Literature concepts wherever they occur.

The table for common auxiliaries of Language was not so enumerative in the UDC editions published before 1993. 1993 edition contains 13 pages of Language tables. By all means this is a very exhaustive table for Languages in the world. This table serves as the source for the subdivisions of class 811 Languages and class 821 Literatures of individual Languages. Language auxiliary has multipurpose application. Linguistic form of a document is represented by using the symbol = (equals) and Language study and theory of Languages are represented in Language class by taking subdivisions from the table without using the connecting symbol=. Relative examples make the multipurpose application more clear.

1. Textbook of Physics in English 53=111
2. English grammar 811.111'36
3. Telugu Language encyclopedia 811.572.24(03)

In the example 1 the subject of the book is Physics and the Language in which it is written is English. Hence the number is 53=111 (=111 taken from Language Table). In the example 2 the subject of the book is English Language and the linguistic study is grammar. Hence the number is 811.111'36. Here three components are used one is languages from the class 811 languages. There is a note under this class which reads as the subdivisions of 811 can be derived from = 1/=9 (Table 1c. Languages) by substituting a point for the equals sign. Hence English Language has a notation 811.111 (instead of = 111, .111 is used as per the note) =111 is taken from the Language table. There is also another note under 811 class which reads as Further specification of individual Languages or Language groups by adding '0/'44 and/or -2/-26. Accordingly, the specification required for this title English Language is grammar. This has a number '36. Hence the compound number 811.111'36 for the title: English Language grammar.

In the example 3. Telugu Language encyclopedia, Telugu Language number is not listed in the 811 class as such. However, Dravidian Languages is represented under the number 811.57 (.57 is taken from = 57 Language table). Telugu Language happens to be a Dravidian Language the number must be got from = 57 table. = 572.24 is the number given to the Telugu Language in this table. Hence Telugu Language number is derived as 811.572.24 (= replaced by. as per the above note under 811 class). Encyclopedia is a Form auxiliary and is got from the Form table as (03). The compound number for the title Telugu Language encyclopedia will be 811.572.24(03).

There are drastic changes in the Main class 8 in 1993 edition when compared to the earlier editions of the UDC.

Practising librarians may experience serious difficulties in making changes to the existing numbers (classification) by using

1993 edition. The problems associated with reclassification are also encountered with this class.

g) *Common auxiliaries of Form*: Symbol (0...)

A very important common auxiliary to represent a Form of the document is introduced in the UDC. With the help of the Form symbol,books can be separated by virtue of the treatment of the subjects concerned and the levels of books like student/ textbooks, advanced, research, general type etc. Books can also be separated by their size, condition, printed or otherwise etc. and also the contents of data, tables, diagrams etc.

Like in Language auxiliary, tables are provided for various subdivisions of this auxiliary. Though many forms of documents are to be represented by using this auxiliary, literary forms are not included in this auxiliary. They are specially classed under Literature (82-1/-9). Another important feature of this auxiliary is that it contains subdivisions of both common auxiliaries and special auxiliaries.

The divisions and subdivisions of this table can both be represented as dependent and independent auxiliary depending on the need. As mentioned under auxiliary tables earlier, forms of documents if to be represented without giving priority to the subject i.e. Handbooks - Physics can be given importance to handbook, then this form division is an independent auxiliary. The number would be 035:53. Whereas if the subject is more important than the form then the number is reversed and the Form is dependent auxiliary: 53(035).

Examples of Form common auxiliaries and its subdivisions :

(0)

(01) Bibliographies

(02) Books in general

(03) Reference Works.

....

....

....

Special auxiliary subdivisions.

(0.0) Physical features, production and use characteristics

(0.02) Documents according to physical, external form

(0.03) Documents according to method of production.

(0.04) Documents according to stage of production

(0.05) Documents for particular kinds of user

(0.06) Documents according to level of presentation and availability

(0.07) Supplementary matter issued with a document.

(0.08) Separately issued supplements or parts of documents.

The above special auxiliary subdivisions and their sub subdivisions can be attached to the common auxiliaries of Form and their subdivisions to form an exhaustive compound number.

Illustrations

Readers digest World Atlas large size. 084.402.12

08 Collective Works

084 Pictorial documents Graphic documents

084.4 Atlases

084.402 (.02 documents according to Physical size)

084.402.12 Large size documents (.021.2 large documents)

Mcgraw-Hill Encyclopedia of Science & Technology Medium sized. 5/6 (031.021.3)

5 Sciences

6 Applied Sciences. Technology, Medicine.

5/6 Science and Technology (5 and 6 are consecutive classes. Hence separated by /)

(0..) Form common auxiliary

(03) Reference Books

(031) Encyclopedia.

Special auxiliary division of common auxiliary (0.)

(0.02) Documents according to Physical and external form - size.

(0.021) Scope and size

(0.021.3) Medium size

(031.021.3) Medium sized encyclopedia.

The special auxiliary subdivisions are to be attached to the main common auxiliary. In this case main auxiliary is (03) and its subdivisions (0.021.3) is attached to (031), then the number becomes (031.021.3) for medium sized encyclopedia. Since it is a dependent common auxiliary in this case, the Form auxiliary is to be attached to the main class. Here main class is a compound class 5/6. Consequently the title Mcgraw Hill encyclopedia of Science and Technology medium sized edition will have a classification number as 5/6 (031.021.3). In case the size of the book is ignored then the number could be 5/6 (031). The Form common auxiliary is very much used in reference books where the forms are multifarious.

Throughout this Form table, cross references are indicated to the main tables of the classification. These serve to remind users that the auxiliary denotes the Form in which the material is presented, not works about that Form.

In a special library, the collection consists of advanced level books such as conferences/symposia/seminars proceedings, design data books, manuals, theses, lecture notes, bibliographies, reports etc. Hence the 'form' auxiliary is very much in use in special libraries.

Proceedings of a conference will have a number (063). This number is attached to the main class number of the document. Machine tool design conference - proceedings will have a number 621.9(063) and an University thesis on machine tool design will have 621.9 (043.2) in which (043.2) is for theses. academic theses.

The provision of additional cards under Form division enable the library to compile a list of books in individual forms separately and also to distinguish the levels of the subjects. In addition, such a provision enables access to the catalogue through Form division route. An illustration will make matters further clear :

All theses in a library are classified first according to their individual subject and a form division (043.2) is attached to each number. While preparing catalogue cards additional cards are prepared for the form - thesis i.e. (043.2) and filed under (043.2) sequence in the classified catalogue. In a machine readable catalogue, the database is indexed as per the form division (043.2) and other form divisions also. A search by (043.2) in classified catalogue and database reveals the number and nature of university theses available in a library. Likewise, number and nature of other forms available in a library can be obtained. With the help of the 'form common auxiliary' a classification within a classification is possible. The first classification being subject and the second classification is the Form of the document. As this Form division plays an important role in the classification scheme, some more examples are worth considering :

Examination papers- Physics 53(079.1)

Instruction manuals- Computers 681.3(076)

Agriculture - Statistical tables 63(083.4)

Selective bibliography on Labour problems 331(01) or 331(048.1)

Corrosion atlas 620.193(034.4)

History of Physics 53 (09)

h) *Common auxiliary of Place*: Symbol (1/9)

To represent the subject belonged to a particular location or place, Place auxiliaries are used. A separate schedule of Place auxiliaries is given from the page No.21 to 65 in the main part of the UDC text. As common to all auxiliary divisions, the Place auxiliary is placed at the end of the main class number. In addition to geographical locations, representation of zones like hot, tropical, mountains, plains, deserts, oceans, seas, rivers, waterways, Islands is also given in the schedules. Continents are treated as main classes and the countries are subdivisions and the places in the countries are sub subdivisions. Like in language auxiliary, the Place auxiliaries form a basis for the parallel division of 913/919 and 93/99 by deleting the brackets and prefixing 91 and 9 respectively. Example 914.4 Geography of France. 91 Geography and (44) France and 944 History of France again 44 derived from (44) France. The table of place auxiliary has the following broad divisions.

(1) Place and space in general

(2) Physiographic designation

(20) Ecosphere

(21) Land areas

(211/213) Climatic zones

(23) Above sea level. Mountains

(24) Below sea level subterranean

(25) Natural flat ground

(26) Oceans, seas and interconnections

(28) Inland waters

(3) Places of the ancient world.

(4) Places of the Modern World.

Special auxiliary divisions

(1-0/-9) Boundaries and spatial forms of various kinds.

These are used in the form in which they are enumerated.

For example (1-051) Elongated areas. Strips. They are also used to qualify any of the concepts listed in the table Roman empire (37-44)

Illustrations

Town planning in USA 711.4(73)

7 The Arts.

71 Physical Planning

711 Urban, rural planning

711.4 Town planning

(7) North America

(73) USA

World of Learning 378.4(100)

3 Social Sciences

37 Education

378 Higher education

378.4 Universities. University Colleges

(100) World. International.

Dances of South India. 793(548)

We can also coin a number for South India as (540-14) (540) India, (1-14) South. Since the number is already enumerated it is better to confine to the scheduled number for the purpose of consistency.

i) *Common auxiliaries of ethnic grouping and Nationality:(=..)*

This auxiliary relates to the aspect of Race and Nationality of a subject. The connecting symbol differs from Language common auxiliary by putting equal to sign within brackets. The common auxiliaries are derived mainly from the common auxiliaries of Language. Hence the common symbol =. This auxiliary needs to be used only in exceptional cases where the stress is on Race and Nationality. For example a title like 'Customs and Traditions of Indians' needs the common auxiliary to represent Indians Nationality (=1.540) Indians.

Like Language table, this table also contains common auxiliary subdivisions and special auxiliary subdivisions.

This number happens to be for Nationality and the numbers from Place table are used to represent ethnic groups. For giving physical location, the numbers from Place table are taken and for people numbers from Nationality table are taken.

To illustrate the point:

Science and Technology in India will have a number 5/6 (540).

Scientific practices of Indians will have a number 5 (=1.540).

You will notice the difference in the Form division for Place and Nationality, though the number 540 is mnemonic.

For Place it is used within brackets and for Nationality it is used with prefix = and within brackets.

Illustrations

1. Ethnology of Red Indians 572.9(=81/=82)

57	Biological Sciences
572	Anthropology
572.9	Social anthropology. Ethnology (=81/=82) North American Indians.

2. History of ancient Romans

937	(=1.37)
93/99	History
937	History of ancient Rome (to 476AD) (=1.37) ancient Romans.)

j.*Common auxiliaries of Time*: Symbol "..."

The common auxiliaries of Time denotes the date, point of time or range of time of a subject represented by the main UDC number. The date refers to the subject of the document and not to the publication date of the document which is taken care of by cataloguing process. In addition to double quotation, + and - are used for AD and BC dates respectively. Both these are prefixed to the dates as per AD and BC. Decimal point is used to represent smaller time divisions like minutes, seconds etc.. However the decimal point should not be mistaken with the point used after every third digit in UDC number. Only Arabic numerals are used to represent the time. This auxiliary is very much used in Religion, History, Geography and other subjects where development activity is involved in relation to a period of time.

For example : Hinduism in 12th Century

294.5 "11" (i.e. 1101 - 1199 AD)

Time elements can be fully represented with the help of decimal points. The dates are denoted by citing the ordinary calendar notation in the order year-month-date-hours-minutes-seconds.

"1995.06.12.16.46.43" 12th June 1995 at 16 hrs 46 minutes and 43 seconds.

Twentieth century Physics : 53"19"

Physics 53

20th century "19"

Centuries are represented in 2 digits and decades in 3 digits as:

20th century "19"

1960s "196" (The nineteen sixties)

Ranges of centuries or decades or years may be denoted by the initial and final figures linked with the stroke.

"04/14" 5th to 15 centuries

"1939/1945" period of the Second World War

"625/627" Glacial and post glacial periods.

When a date is undetermined it is indicated by...954 ".../19" Indian history upto the end of 20th century.

This table is enumerated exhaustively in 1993 edition. Depth schedules are available for the minute divisions of the day i.e. sunset period, dusk, dawn etc. also 7 pages are devoted to this table in the UDC Main schedules.

k) *Subject specifications by notations from non-UDC sources* Symbols * and A/Z

Here * and Alphabetization devices are the two devices. The *is for the notation which is not an authorised UDC number. The * may follow a UDC number to introduce a word, symbol or number from a non UDC source, which is added in order to specify a subject. In such combination the asterisk serves to mark their separation from the UDC numbers.

1. Refrigerant Freon 28. 621.564.2 *Fr 28.
2. Alloy Inconel 8600 669.24'26* INCONEL 600. (Nickel Chromium alloy)

In the example 1. A general number is given for all refrigerants as 621.564.2. Here a specific refrigerant Freon 28 is to be represented. This is done with the help of * as above.

In the example 2. Inconel is a trade name of Nickel, Chromium alloy. The number for nickel chromium alloys is 669.24 '26 (Nickel alloys 669.24 and chromium alloys 669.26). Inconel 600 is to be represented hence the * is used.

A/Z Direct alphabetical specification.

Alphabetical device is a common device used in many classification schemes. It is a flexible device and can be used liberally. This can be at the convenience of the classifier. However the classifier shall maintain the consistency in specifying the number of letters to a standard length. Suppose we have a name like Tiruchirapalli to be represented by this device we can not use such a lengthy name as it is. Some sort of abbreviation is required such as first four letters as long as there is no ambiguity on the four letters in the existing classification number.

Alphabetical device follows the main UDC number. For example a title 'Computer programming in COBOL' can be represented by 681.3.06 COBOL or 681.3.06COBO or 681.3.06C (Full name,abbreviated name (limited to 4 letters) and single letter for abbreviation. But ambiguity occurs in the case of the title 'Computer programming in C language' where it is represented as 681.3.06C. This clashes with the above title when only one letter is used. To avoid such conflict it is better to standardise the abbreviation to either three or four letters. We can give a number of examples where the ambiguity is likely to occur.

Biography of Jawaharlal Nehru.

929 Jawaharlal or 929 Nehru or 929 N.

Biography of Napoleon 929 N:

City of Madras (548.1-25 Madras) (548.1-25M)

City of Madurai (548.1-25 Madurai) (548.1-25M)

Examples of alphabetical device:

State of Haryana (545.2 HAR)

Thermal Power Station - Vijayawada

621.311.22 Vijayawada

62 Engineering. Technology in general

621 Mechanical engineering

621.3 Electrical Engineering

621.311 Power generation

621.311.2 Power Stations

621.311.22 Thermal Power Stations

Vijayawada - Alphabetical device

We have so far dealt with independent common auxiliaries.

Now student is introduced to the dependent common auxiliaries.

2.2 DEPENDENT COMMON AUXILIARIES

There are three dependent common auxiliaries which can be used as suffixes to the main UDC number. These are .00 Points of view, - 03,-05 common auxiliaries and -1/-9, .01/.09 and '0/9' special auxiliaries.

a) Common auxiliaries of point of view

Symbol .00

This common auxiliary helps in sharpening the focus of the subject treated in a book. i.e. with what point of view the book is written: concept, theory, function, activity, process etc. They can be applied anywhere in the schedule. Though the auxiliary is available, it is advisable to use it only when a point of view facet is needed to be represented in order to achieve an useful differentiation of a concept denoted by a main number.

Theoretical Physics 53.001

Experimental Physics 53.001.4

Digital computers 681.32

Digital Computers operational aspect 681.32.004.

It is advisable to use a different class when a concept is available there. For example : Engineering - accounts points of view is classified as 62:657.47 instead of using .003 Economics and financial point of view since there is a difference in the main class 657.47 Accountancy and dependent auxiliary .003 points of view. In case of 657.47 a separate catalogue card can be provided under the class 657.47 to direct the user to know the books on accountancy and accounts point of view. But in case of .003 no catalogue card can be provided as it is a dependent auxiliary. Therefore it is to be noted that when there is a need to represent the concepts in a compound number it is to be given a separate class number so that a separate subject sequence can be maintained under that class number. Alternately only point of view may be represented for the less important concept.

Illustrations:

By products of Chemical Industry 66.002.67

66 Chemical Industry.

.002 Practical points of view. Production

.002.6 Results of processes. Products

.002.68 By products.

Work study from trade union point of view - 65.015.000.331.105.44.

65 Management

65.01 Methods and Methodology

65.015 Work study and analysis.

.000 General approach.

(Here subdivision is as per 0/9 Main classes)

Under .000.0/.9 there is a note that .000.0/.9 ≅ 0/9.

(Following the number .000. the main classes are added for the subject approach.

331.105.44 Trade Unions.

When this is attached to the above points of view number.000 then it will be .000.331.105.44. This should be attached to the main class 65.015 to make it trade union point of view. Here two separate main classes are linked up with the help of points of view auxiliary. The two main classes are 65.015 and 331.105.44 for the subjects work study and trade unions respectively. In the present case trade unions is only an approach aspect.

Hence it is used as supplementary to the main class 65.015.

Likewise the subject approach is specified by the respective class attached to the points of view auxiliary

b. **Common auxiliaries of materials**: Symbol - 03.

This concept has been added in the recent revisions of the UDC i.e. from 1985 onwards. a special auxiliary - is selected for this purpose and 03 is earmarked for materials. As in the case of other auxiliaries, here also materials are secondary to the subject. When material aspect is primary then it is classified under the concerned class.

A separate schedule is provided enumerating various materials. This auxiliary is a dependent auxiliary and as such can not be treated by itself as a subject. This is always suffixed to the main class. For example: Mining of Coal. 622 - 032.35.

When more than one material is to be represented then the second material is represented by ' instead of repeating - 03.

For example :

Polyester and glass fibre - 036.674'752

- 036.674 Polyester fibres

- 037.52 Glass fibres.

in the above example glass fibre is represented as '752 taken from -037.52. Here - 03 is replaced by ' (apostrophe) and the remaining number 752 is attached to form '752.

After enumerating maximum number of materials, the schedule provides - 039 class for all other materials which are not enumerated in the schedules. Though the materials listed in the schedule are applicable throughout the main classes, they are generally applicable to 66 and 67 classes. Materials table is divided as materials, naturally occurring mineral materials, materials of organic origin, macromolecular materials etc.

Illustrations

Ceramic insulating materials 621.315.61-033.65

621.3 Electrical Engineering

621.31 Electric Power generation

621.315 Electric Power Transmission

621.315.6 Insulating materials. Insulators ....

621.315.61 Insulating materials

-03 Materials auxiliary

-033 Manufactured mineral based materials

-033.6 Ceramics. Pottery. Clayware general

-033.65 Special ceramic object for Electrical purposes.

Plastic Electrical insulation materials 621.315.61 - 036.5

621.315.61 Insulating materials

-036 Macromolecular Materials. Rubbers and Plastics.

- 036.5 Plastics in general.

Library stacks - wooden shelves - Preservation

022.43 - 035.3:025.9

02 Librarianship

022 Library site, building, premises, equipment

022.4 Organisation of book storage

022.43 Storage stacks

-03 Materials auxiliary

-035 Materials of Organic Origin

-035.3 Wood. Timber. Logwood etc.

025 Library administration

025.9 Maintenance. Preservation.

c) Common auxiliaries of Persons and Personal characteristics: Symbol - 05.

Like materials auxiliary, common auxiliary for persons is also introduced from 1985 onwards. As in materials, this common auxiliary is used as secondary to the main subject. This common auxiliary denotes the persons or their characteristics but not things or disciplines according to personal applications. This common auxiliary is applicable throughout the main tables.

A separate schedule enumerating various divisions of this auxiliary is provided. This common auxiliary is particularly useful in identifying the books on persons concerned with concepts or professions. Earlier editions of the UDC did not provide this auxiliary and as such it was not possible to bring out the difference between the profession and the professional. For example there was no difference in treatment of books on Buddhism and Buddhists as both were classified under 294.3. Engineers and Engineering were classified under 62 only. Now with this auxiliary, books on Buddhism are classified under 294.3 and books on Buddhists under 294.3-05. Books on Engineering are classified under 62 and on Engineers under 62-051.

-05 is broadly divided as

-051 Persons as agents, doers, practitioners professionals

-052 Persons as targets, clients, users (studied, served).

-053 Persons according to ages, age groups. Children, Young, adults, middle aged, old, etc.

-054 Persons according to ethnic characteristics, nationality, citizenship etc.

-055 Persons according to sex and kinship.

-056 Persons according to constitution, health, disposition, hereditary or other trails.

-057 Persons according to occupation, work, livelihood

-058 Persons according to social class, civil status.

One or more subdivisions can be used by attaching the number of that subdivision with - (hyphen). For example : Female adolescent engineers 62-053.6-055.2

This common auxiliary can be combined with other common auxiliaries. For example: Indian Mathematics Prodigy 51-056.45 (540)

This common auxiliary is a dependent common auxiliary and needs to be attached only to the main UDC number.

Illustrations:

Scientists of the 19th century.

50-051 "18"

5 Mathematics and Natural Sciences

50 Generalities about the pure science

-05 Common auxiliary for persons and their characteristics

-051 Professionals

50-051 Professionals of Science (Scientists)

" " Common auxiliary for Time

"18" 19th Century (1800-1899)

50-051 "18" Scientists of 19th Century.

Nurses in India. 616-051 (540)

61 Medicine

616 Pathology

-051 Persons as agents (Studying, Serving etc)

616-051 Medical Staff, Doctors, Nurses.

(540) India

616-051 (540) Nurses in India.

Wages of industrial workers in Great Britain.

331.2-058.234.2 (410)

33 Economics

331 Labour. Employment. Work

331.2 Salaries, Wages, Remuneration.

-05 Common auxiliary for persons

-058 Persons according to Social class or status

058.2 Persons of particular class according to ownership of production.

-058.23 Persons of particular levels in capitalist Society.

-058.234 Members of the proletariat. Working class.

-058.234.2 Industrial Workers.

331.2-058.234.2 Wages of industrial workers

(410) Great Britain

331.2-058.234.2 (410) Wages of industrial workers of Great Britain.

2.3 SPECIAL AUXILIARY SUBDIVISIONS

Special auxiliary subdivisions are of three types a)-1/-9 b).01/.09 c) '0/'9.

By their nature, the special auxiliaries are created for specific applications in that part of the main tables for which they are designed and represent a concept of recurring nature.

Unlike the common auxiliary signs and subdivisions of Section I, in the special auxiliaries the same notation may be used with different meanings in different parts of main tables. However, under one main number and its subdivisions the notation denotes the same recurrent concept with the same meaning.

a)-*1/-9*

For example 271-1 denotes Religious vocation

Whereas 62-1 denotes General characteristics of machines. thus -1 has different meaning in these two classes.

However, in 271.1-1 and 271.974-1, -1 has the same meaning. While it is Bendictnes religious vocation in 271.1-1, it is Ursulines religious vocation in 271.974-1. This is what is meant by the statement that under the same main number (271 in this case) the recurring concept 'religious vocation' is denoted by the same special auxiliary -1.

In the main class 62, -1 has the same meaning throughout 62/69 except at 633/635, 66,678 and 687.

Thus

Characteristics of Electric Motors 621.313.13 -1

Characteristics of Hydraulic machines 621.22 -1

Characteristics of Boilers 621.18-1

will have special auxiliary -1 etc. attached to their individual main numbers. (Here the General Characteristic is recurring)

In 82 main class, -1 has different meaning Poems, Verses. The meaning is same throughout Literature class. English poetry, Russian Poetry and other languages poetry will have the same special auxiliary attached to the Main Literature class. 821.111-1 English Poetry, 821.161.1-1 Russian Poetry.

One will find this special auxiliary in many classes throughout the schedules. However care should be taken to not to confuse with other common auxiliaries starting with - sign.

Illustrations

Trouble shooting in electronic devices. 621.38-7

621.3 Electrical Engineering

621.38 Electronics. Electronic devices

- Special auxiliary at 62

-7 Servicing, maintenance.

Juvenile literature in Telugu. 821.572.24-93

821 Literature

= Language common auxiliary

= 57 Dravidian Languages

= 572 Central branch

= 572.24 Telugu

821.572.24 Telugu literature

- Special auxiliary under 82

-9 Various other genres

-93 Juvenile literature

b) The point nought series .01/.09 are much more detailed than -1/-9, providing sets and subsets of recurrent concepts such as aspect studies, activities, processes,plant and equipment.

The very structure of this special auxiliary indicates that

this is a subdivision like a decimal point of an integer. All the decimal points of an integer are thus used to denote subsets/ subdivisions of sets/main divisions.

Unlike the earlier special auxiliary, this is quite common to all the classes where the recurring aspects, processes and activities are grouped at the main class and represented by this auxiliary i.e. .01/.09.

In Chemistry class 54, the aspects of Chemistry such as chemical substances, chemical composition, preparation, synthesis, analysis etc. are common for all the disciplines of Chemistry, like inorganic chemistry, physical chemistry, organic chemistry . Hence they are listed at the beginning of the class 54.

Thus 54.022 Structure of atoms

544.022 Structure in Physical Chemistry

546.18.022 Structure of Phosphorus.

547.022 Structure of organic compounds

549.022 Structure of minerals.

In all the above .022 is structure.

In Physics 53 class, special auxiliary .0/.9 are listed at the beginning. For example .08 is for theory of measurement and Measurement methods.

53.08 Measurement

532.5.08 Flow measurement (532.5 Fluid Mechanics)

533.6.08 Air flow measurement (533.6 Aerodynamics)

534.08 Acoustical measurement

535.08 Optical measurement

536.08 Heat measurement

....

....

....

539.08 Nuclear, Atomic measurement

In Medicine class 61, special auxiliary subdivisions .0/.9 are not the same in all the subdivisions of 61. Hence Medicine class should be treated separately for this purpose. For example, .018 is histology under 611 anatomy, it is hormones under 612 Physiology.

Special auxiliary divisions are abundantly used in almost all main classes. By virtue of their nature, they are listed under each main class wherever the auxiliaries need to be used. Because of this reason, they have not been isolated and listed under a separate table like the other common auxiliaries. Hence this auxiliary can be treated as a subdivision or part of individual main class in which it is listed.

Illustrations:

High Voltage circuit breakers. 621.316.57.027.3

621.3 Electrical Engineering

621.31 Power Generation, Supply and control.

621.316 Distribution and regulation of Power.

621.316.5 Opening and closing of circuits.
circuit breakers. Holders.

621.316.57 Power circuit breakers

.0 Special auxiliary subdivisions

.02 Type and range of current, power, voltage (listed under 621.3) etc

.027 Voltage. Tension

.027.3 High Voltage. High Tension.

621.316.57.027.3 High Voltage Circuit Breakers.

Thermal processes and plant in steel making. 669.14.046.

669 Metallurgy

669.1 Ferrous Metallurgy

669.14 Steel in general

.0 Special auxiliary subdivision.

.04 Heat treatment (listed under 66 class as well as under 669 class)

.046 Thermal processes and plant

669.14.046 Thermal processes and plant in steel making.

c) The apostrophe series '1/'9 are mainly synthetic or integrative in function and denote compound subjects by compound notation. They are sometimes fully listed, but elsewhere are derived from main numbers by parallel subdivision.

The purpose of this special auxiliary is to save digits and make notation brief. However, this can happen only in cases where the concepts are in the same array. For example in Metallurgy class where alloys are to be represented, this auxiliary division is in use. Naturally an alloy involves more than one metal, it is a lengthy number if all the metals are to be represented in one compound number with the help of common auxiliaries. Copper- Zinc - Tin - Vanadium alloys: Notation for this title in the normal way looks like 669.35:669.5 : 669.6:669.292

By making use of apostrophe we can simplify this number to look like 669.35'5'6'292. We could lessen the number by 12 characters (spaces) in this way.

Invariably an alloy contains more than one metal/ element. Hence alloys require such a notation. A clever foresight by the people who have introduced this auxiliary into the UDC . To this special auxiliary, another special auxiliary - can also be attached to represent further aspects. For example : Low alloy steels of nickel and chromium will have a number 669.15 '24'26 - 194 where 669.15-194 is for low alloy steels. 669.24 nickel 669.26 chromium.

In addition to 669 class, the special auxiliaries ' are found under 329,547,628,8,81,903 Classes but every time with specific purpose and for specific application.

In addition to main classes, the special auxiliaries ' are used in common auxiliary tables also.

Illustrations

Preparation of acid alcohol esters. 547.29'26.07

Here two special auxiliaries are used (' and .0)

54 Chemistry

547 Organic Chemistry

547.29 Acids

547.26 Alcohols

547.29'26 Acid alcohols esters.

54.07 Preparation

547.29'26.07 Preparation of acid alcohol esters.

French language usage spoken and written form.

811.133.1'271.1

811 Languages

811.13 Romance languages

811.133.1 French Languages

' Special auxiliary

' 2/'44 Subject fields and facets of linguistics.

'27 Sociolinguistics. Usage of languages.

'271 Usage and purity of languages

'271.1 Correct usage of spoken and written forms.

811.133.1'271.1 French Language usage of spoken and written forms.

Heat treatment of quenched metal alloys of cobalt, iron.

669.14'25-156.04

This is a typical example where all three special auxiliary subdivisions (-1/-9, .01/.09 '1/'9) are in use.

669.14 Alloys of iron

669.25 Cobalt

669.14'25 Iron cobalt alloys. ('is in use)

- 156 Quenched metals (- is in use)

.04 Heat treatment (.0 is in use)

669.14'25-156.04 Heat treatment of Quenched metal alloys of cobalt iron.

We have discussed all the common auxiliaries, special auxiliaries and their applications in various main classes to sharpen the foci of various subjects in their depth. Now we shall go in to the main schedules of various subjects in the universe.

3

Main Tables

This chapter covers broadly the scope of each main class and its contents as envisaged by the UDC.

3.0 CLASS 0 - GENERALIA

For any classification scheme there should be a general class to accommodate all the subjects that are not covered by the other subject classes. This general class called Generalia with notation 0 is concerned with knowledge in general, forms of Communication and in particular writing and standardisation. Subjects relating to Library and Information science are included in this class. Numbers 01/09 are assigned to this class. Common auxiliaries of Form division numbers are used to express the subjects of this class in depth. For example Newspapers are listed in common auxiliaries Form division as a form. But as a main class same subdivision should be taken from the Form division and make 054 as main class. It is to be noted that Form division and Generalia class are one and the same in their scope except that they are used with ( ) and without ( ) in Form division and main classes respectively.

3.1 CLASS 1:PHILOSOPHY. PSYCHOLOGY.

Covers theory of knowledge, principles of knowledge and manifestations of knowledge which are fused into topics such as

Metaphysics, Epistemology, Logic, Reasoning, Psychology and Ethics. History of Philosophy is treated in class 14. Philosophers and their doctrines should be given numbers with relation to the subject of the philosopher by which he is recognised. For example Karl Marx philosophy is classified under number 141.82:33 and Leninism under 141.82:32.

Psychology is subordinate to Philosophy. Hence it is a very big class by itself. A special auxiliary division .0 is provided here to express recurring concepts concerning to Psychology. Various forms, principles, philosophies, theories of Psychology are provided with numbers here. Common auxiliary of persons - 05 can be used to individualise the Psychology aspect. Psychology of adults :159.922.6-053.8.

Special auxiliary subdivision can be used with the Persons common auxiliary.

Topics related to Education are given Education class number. Racial and national Psychology are linked up to the table of common auxiliaries of 'ethnic grouping and nationality'.

Special auxiliary subdivisions '.0' series are provided in 17 class: Moral Philosophy. Ethics. 18 and 19 classes are vacant, a provision for future expansion. Classes 11 to 17 are occupied and allotted to various disciplines of Philosophy.

3.2 CLASS 2: RELIGION. THEOLOGY.

Covers subjects relating to religion, religious practices, religious places, religious scriptures, religious doctrines. Considerable enumeration is provided for all the aspects of religions of the world. Naturally, Christian religion has been represented in a very elaborate manner. The other religions are covered modestly. However a depth schedule can be designed wherever necessary by using the subdivisions provided under Christian religion.

21 class covers Natural Theology which encompasses religious questions from a purely philosophical and rational point of view irrespective of any particular religion. The topics include God, Proof of existence of God, theism, atheism,

rationalism, scepticism non existence of God, Religion and Science, Eternity, immortality, Anthropomorphism etc.

A separate class 22 is allotted to 'Bible, Holy scripture'. This class is very exhaustive and covers all aspects of Bible: its testaments, Concordances, Criticism, Commentaries etc by various religious Priests. Classes 23 to 28 are devoted to Christianity. Christian Churches, Christian Worship, Christian theology, Christian priests, Christian sacred places, Christian religious practices etc.,

Class 29 is allotted to non Christian religions: Hinduism, Buddhism, Jainism, Zoroastrianism, Judaism, Islam and newer religions like Babism.

Special auxiliary subdivisions '.0' are to be used at 22 and '-' at 264 and 271.

Use of synthesis through symbol ≅ is very predominant in this class as the subdivisions of Religions are quite common. Instead of repeating the subdivisions under each class, ≅ is indicated to make subdivisions analogous to the subdivisions given under the preceding class. For example under 291 comparative study and history of religions, listed are the concepts such as nature, origin, doctrines, dogmas, objects etc of religions. The same concepts are to be repeated if the same are to be enumerated under individual religion. Instead of that under each religion there is an instruction to subdivide the number analogous to the class 291 for representing the concepts of 291 class. Therefore the concept of nature or origin of Vedism shall have a number 294.111.1 (294.11≅ 291) and priests of Vedism i.e. Brahmins shall have a number 294.116.1 (291.61 Priests). This is a clever arrangement depicting mnemonic nature of the classification system.

Abundant cross references to other classes are provided at various places of this class.

3.3 CLASS 3: SOCIAL SCIENCES.

Major classes covered under this main class include Sociology, Political Science, Economics, Law, Education, and

Public Administration. All these subclasses are further divided to represent minute subjects under each class.

Tables of Common auxiliaries of Persons (-05) and Ethnic groupings (=..) are very much relevant for use in this class. Special auxiliary subdivisions of .07 and .08 only are listed under 3 and as such are applicable throughout 3 main class and its subdivisions. Special auxiliary subdivisions .01/.06 and .09 are listed at individual classes representing different concepts relevant to the concerned individual class. For example 321.02 represents form of Political activity, 303.02 General features of research, 314.02 Sources of demographic data, 332.02 Economic Policy, Planning etc. and 37.02 General Questions of didactics and method of education. It is evident from these examples that Special auxiliary divisions in this particular class do not function in the same way as they function in other classes.

In this class there is a need to use a number of auxiliary tables to express a variety of concepts in combination and in individual circumstances. The combination of concepts may be from different main classes or within the same main class. For example a) Farmers in feudal societies, will have a combination of concepts within the same class: 316.343.64:316.323.5. (316 class). b) Organisation of unemployment statistics will have a combination of concepts within the same main class '3' : 311.3:331.56 (31 and 33 classes). c) Spread of Zionism through broadcasting will have a combination of concepts from two different main classes 32 and 65 as 323.13.019.5:654.19.

In class 39 Ethnology, the common auxiliary (=..) Ethnic groups, Nationality will be very much in use. Also the main class 2 Religion is in abundant use here.

3.4 CLASS 5. MATHEMATICS AND NATURAL SCIENCES.

Classes 5 and 6 are very closely related and the UDC is very strong in enumerating these two classes to its full coverage of subjects in the universe. By virtue of these enumerations, UDC has got distinction of its application in special libraries especially in science and technology. Though the length of class numbers is long, the full advantage is taken to use all common and special auxiliaries provided in the classification scheme.

Class 5 represents all sciences in the order first inanimate or physical sciences followed by animate or life sciences. A separate section is provided for Environmental sciences as this subject is gaining much importance in the world now. Mother of all sciences, Mathematics is given 51 class. Computational aspect is given a class 519.6 whereas Computer technology and science is classified under 681.3.

Mathematics 51 class is divided into 511 Number theory, 512 Algebra, 514 Geometry – 519.6 Computational methods. Special auxiliary subdivision - (hyphen) provided at 51 is applicable throughout 51 class. 513 class is vacant. Special auxiliary subdivisions '.0' are listed at the appropriate place so to be used in those subclasses only. For example, 514.01 Foundation of geometry; .01 is applicable only in 514 and its subdivisions to represent foundation concept. Foundation of solid geometry will be represented as 514.7.01. 516 class is also vacant and so also 518 class. Computer programming listed at 519.6 is concerned with mathematical aspect only and hence should not be confused with Computer programming techniques and languages listed under 681.3. In the same way Mathematical aspects of Control systems are treated under 519.71 and Control systems engineering at 681.5.

52 Astronomy. Special auxiliaries - (hyphen) listed at 52 applicable to 52 thro' 524. This class draws some of its subdivisions from 62 class in regard to instruments, devices, current range, frequency and other aspects. Hence the special auxiliaries -1/-7 are to be subdivided analogous to 62 class.

While Geodetic Surveying is included in this class, Military Surveying is located in 623 Military Engineering. Chronology, Calendar, Time aspects are included in 529 class.

53 Physics is subdivided into 530 Basic principles, 531 Mechanics, 535 Optics, 536 Heat and Thermodynamics, 537 Electricity, 539 Physical nature of matter. 538 is vacant.Theoretical and experimental aspects of all the above subjects are covered under 53. Application aspect of these

subjects are covered under 62 Engineering as Engineering is nothing but applied science. Thereby 531 Mechanics is theoretical and experimental and 621.01 is Applied mechanics or Mechanical Engineering. In the same way 536 is Heat and 621.1 is Heat engineering (Thermal engineering) 537 Electricity and 621.3 is Electrical Engineering.

539 covers Atomic, Nuclear and Molecular physics and 621.039 is Nuclear Engineering.

In 53 class, the special auxiliaries - and .0 are abundantly used. .0 divisions are listed at 53 and are applicable throughout 53 class. Aerodynamic flow measurement is 533.6.08 and Heat measurement is 536.08.

Solid state physics is given a class number 539.3, Principles and properties of solids are to be classified here. Testing of solids, Strength of materials are to be classified under 620.17. There may be a slight confusion as some concepts of solids are given both under 539.3 and 620.17. Therefore it should be noted that books dealing with properties are to be classified under 539.3 and books dealing with testing for the properties should be classified under 620.17. Likewise elastic limit (Property of a solid) is given a number 539.31 and testing of elastic limit should be given a number 620.172.22

54 Chemistry. Treatment of Chemistry is also on similar lines as of 53 Physics class. However, Chemistry has some distinct concepts like properties, substances, compounds, formulae, form of state : solids, liquids, gases and analysis of chemical compounds. Because of these distinct features, special auxiliary divisions - and .0 are widely used to avoid repetition of numbers alongwith repetition of concepts. For example Chemical compounds are classified as 54-3. Compounds of inorganic elements are to be classified 546 - 3 and compounds of organic elements as 547- 3. Here only concepts are repeated but not the notation - 3 which is the same in all three subjects.

Chemistry is subdivided as 542 Practical chemistry 543 Analytical chemistry, 544 Physical chemistry, 546 Inorganic Chemistry and 547 Organic chemistry. All elements of periodic table are enumerated. Compounds of Inorganic and Organic Chemistry are also well enumerated in the schedule.

Special auxiliary ' is also used in this class for synthesizing function applicable to chemical compounds:

Tungsten Carbide 546.78'261

Tungsten 546.78

Carbides 546.261

548/549 Mineralogical Sciences, Crystallography, Mineralogy, deals with crystal structures, minerals and their properties, Mineral compounds.

Mineralogy leads to 55 Earth sciences. This includes Physiography, Terrestrial Physics, Geochemistry, Climatology, Meteorology, Petrology, Economic geology and Hydrology. Special auxiliary .0 is listed in almost all subdivisions and are to be used for those subdivisions only. Common auxiliary table of Place to be used for the representation of regional geology of various places. Common auxiliary table of Time " " to be used for geological time.

557/559 classes are vacant.

56 Paleontology covers Paleobotany, Paleozoology:

Invertebrata and Vertebrata, Sauropsida and Mammalia. This class is a bridge between Geology and Biology. Hence there is a need to consult these classes to represent concepts relevant to them.

Special auxiliary subdivisions .0 are listed at the head of 56 class and are applicable to 561 through 569. The subdivisions of 56 are parallel to 58 and 59 classes.

Paleontology deals with remains of Plant and animal life. Biology deals with life sciences i.e. Living organisms: Plants and animals.

57 Biology deals with life sciences. Aspects common to both Botany and Zoology are dealt in this class. Individual aspects concerning to Botany are treated in Botany and Zoology in Zoology class.

57 Biology class is subdivided into 572 Anthropology 573 General and Theoretical Biology, 574 Ecology, Biogeography, 575 Genetics, 576 Cellular biology, 577 Molecular biology, 578 Virology, 579 Microbiology. Special auxiliary subdivisions .0

are listed at the head of 57 class and are applicable throughout 57.

In 572 Anthropology class, common auxiliaries of Ethnic grouping and Nationality is applicable to extend the aspects of Anthropology

58 Botany class is subdivided into 581 General Botany, 582 Systematic Botany and 583 to 589 are vacant. Special auxiliaries are used in this class. Common auxiliaries of Place and Time need be used to sharpen the focus of subjects concerning to Botany.

59 Zoology is subdivided into 591 General Zoology, 592 Invertebrata, 594 Mollusca. shellfish etc. 595 Articulata, 596 Vertebrata, 597 Fishes 598, Sauropsida and 599 Mammalia.

Special auxiliary subdivisions -2/-9 are used to represent general concepts of Zoology and concepts related to particular animals and classes of animals.

Details of plants and animals in Botany and Zoology respectively are worked out with the help of these special auxiliaries.

Alphabetical device is employed to represent various plants, species, genes etc. For example: Lilies are represented by 582.572.226 LILIES. In case of Zoology also alphabetical device can be employed to specify names of animals and birds. The enumeration provided in the schedules is only to a broad category of animals and not to the individual names. Hence the need for an alphabetical device.

3.5 CLASS 6: APPLIED SCIENCES. MEDICINE. TECHNOLOGY

While 5 is for natural sciences 6 is for Applied sciences.As mentioned earlier 6 is the main strength of the UDC as this is very much used in special libraries of science and engineering. Class 6 is divided to cover all fields of engineering and technology. The broad subdivisions are

61 Medicine

62 Engineering. Technology

63 Agriculture. Animal husbandry

64 Home economics. House keeping

65 Management

66 Chemical Technology

67 Various industries, trades and crafts

68 Industries of finished articles

69 Building trade.

Each subdivision is further subdivided and occupied all decimal points in each subdivision.

61. Human biology is included here. While 57 is for non human biology, 61 is for human biology. Human anatomy, physiology are provided under 61 only and not at 57/59. 61 class covers medical health, diagnosis, disease, treatment and medicines (Pharmacology).

There are a number of concepts common to anatomy, physiology. Hence special auxiliary subdivisions - and .0 are in very much use. Common auxiliaries of Place (1/9) is also in use.

61 class is very exhaustively enumerated. Animal medicine is included in 619 and in 63 Animal husbandry is included. But the classifier should carefully select the class depending on the relevance and requirement of subject.

A speciality of medicine class is that special auxiliary subdivision -00 is used extensively to derive Morbid processes under 616 Pathology -03 used to represent different concepts other than its normal special auxiliary nature i.e. materials and persons. 616 - 3 is for various forms of diseases -00/-09 are completely utilised for 616.

With the above features Medicine class is distinctive from other classes in the UDC.

62.Engineering is applications of various sciences lead to Engineering discipline. Hence, Engineering is dependent on Physics, Chemistry, Geology and is having close connections with various technologies in 67, 68 and 69.

62 class is divided into 10 subclasses to cover all branches of Engineering

620 Materials Testing

621 Mechanical Engg.

622 Mining

623 Military Engg.

624 Civil and Structural Engg.

625 Surface transport Engg.

626/627 Hydraulic / Water Engg.

628 Public Health Engg.

629 Transport vehicle Engg.

Each of these subclasses are subdivided into 620.1/620.9,621.1/621.9......629.1/629.9.

Special auxiliary subdivisions -1/-9 are enumerated at 62 so to apply them to all 62 and its subdivisions from 62/69. Special auxiliary subdivisions .0/.9 are listed under many sections.

Analysis and synthesis of numbers to build up compound numbers is very great in 62 class. Because of this it is very important to apply analysis and synthesis of subjects in their proper context and derive classification numbers. Classifier should be able to distinguish the concepts in their proper perspective and represent them at proper place by proper number. Else the whole exercise may lead to choas and the very classification purpose may be defeated. A point of caution is also necessary. Suppose Minerals and Metals are the subjects that are dealt in various contexts: Mining, Metallurgy and Manufacture. The subject content of a book should be carefully scanned so as to fix the context of the subject. This should be noted in an authority file or a subject index maintained for this purpose. This particular index must be consulted before fixing the context of the subject with relation to similar titles available in the library.

620 Materials testing is very much related to all the classes that follow 621. Due to this reason, this can be understood as a special auxiliary subdivision except that this is to be used with the help of colon and not with .0 as normally used for special

auxiliary subdivisions. All fields of engineering need materials and so its testing. There is every need to use this class for specifying Materials characterisation and Strength of materials.

For example:

Fatigue strength of turbine components : 621-135:620.178.38

Fatigue strength of automobile parts. 629.33:620.178.38

Fatigue strength of mining hoists. 622.67:620.178.38.

621 Mechanical Engineering in general is divided into

621.01 Mechanical Engineering

621.039 Nuclear Engineering

621.1 Steam Engines

621.22 Hydraulics

621.3 Electrical Engineering

621.4 Heat engines (- Steam Engines)

621.5 Pneumatics

621.6 Fluids Handling

621.7 Workshop technology

621.8 Machine elements

621.9 Machine Tools

Subdivisions by .0 at the head of the class do not constitute special auxiliary tables in the normal sense. 621.039 Nuclear Engineering and any subdivisions that follow this number with .0 prefix can be special auxiliaries. An example is 621.039.5.014 Reactor kinetics.

Each of the above subdivisions has their own special auxiliary subdivisions scheduled in their respective classes.

621.1 and 621.22 are Mechanical Engineering subdivisions with similar operations in Thermal and Hydraulic Engineering aspects.

621.3 and 621.38 are Electrical Engineering and Electronics. These classes have a very exhaustive special auxiliary subdivisions to be applicable throughout 621.3 class.

As in 5 Science class, here also the colon is used to represent compound numbers. Use of electricity for various purposes is a natural phenomenon. Hence colon is used to link up this phenomenon with other subjects. Example: Electricity for cooking 621.365:641.535. Television amplifiers 621.375:621.397.

Special common auxiliaries -1/-9 at 62 are applicable throughout 621.3 also.

622 Mining.Topics include extraction of minerals, oils, gas etc. Economics of the minerals is dealt with the help of colon from 33 class. Points of view common auxiliaries also can be used instead of colon to express Economics of mining. Like Profitability of Mining as 622.003.8.

Special common auxiliaries .0,' are provided to permit the expression of compound concepts. - Special common auxiliary is also used but as per -55 in Geology class.

623 Military Engineering covers Military Science and Engineering. Ammunition, artillery, weapons, military transport vehicles armament, Ballistics, armoury are the topics related to Military Engineering. Special auxiliary subdivisions and common auxiliaries are in use.

624 Civil Engineering covers both Civil and Structural Engineering : its practice, methods. 69 is the class where building materials, trades are included. 72 Class is for Architecture and its design of buildings according to purpose. Special auxiliaries and colon combination are used to build compound numbers.

625 Land Transport Engineering: Here design for transportation of all transports i.e., Road, Rail, and Highway are described. Vehicles used for these transport are separately dealt in 629 class : Vehicle engineering. Design and construction of pavements, roads, highways, railway tracks, etc., are included in this class.

626/627 Hydraulic Structures, waterways, water transport, canals, irrigation, ports and harbours, docks, river protection works, Navigation facilities are all covered.

628 Public health engineering covers water for drinking

and its sources and distribution. This also covers water treatment, purification, sewerage, sewage treatment, water pollution, air pollution. 628.9 deals with lighting and illumination engineering, Airconditioning, heating and ventilating for comfort purpose are included here. Engineering aspects of refrigeration and airconditioning are provided at 621.56/.59.

629 Transport Vehicle Engineering . As mentioned earlier, Vehicle characteristics, design and performance of all vehicles : road, rail, water craft, Air and space are included here. Special auxiliaries .0 are used here to cover the common concepts of all the above vehicles. -1/-9 listed at 62 class are used here to represent machine characteristics of vehicles.

63 Class deals with Agriculture, Horticulture, Sericulture, Fishiculture etc. Crops are mentioned in both agriculture and horticulture depending on the treatment of each crop. Plants that are grown in fields are given under agriculture and that are grown in gardens under horticulture. The class also deals with machinery for agriculture, harvesting, protection of crops etc. Plant protection, pesticides, plant pathology, animal husbandry, Livestock, animal breeding, products from animals etc. are the other topics covered in this class.

64 Class is meant for Home economics, Domestic Science, House Keeping. This class deals with integral part of buildings, internal decoration, maintenance of household things and practice in house keeping. Main function of this class is to cover the household activities, preparation of food, recipes, implements used in preparation of food etc. Health and hygienic values of food are dealt in Medicine class. Cookery, meals, household fittings and furnishings and personal requisites including dressmaking, care and protection of clothing and personal cleanliness are the other classes covered here.

65 Management is a major class which has relation with almost all subjects in the schedule of classification. 65 is divided into the following subdivisions.

651 Office Management

654 Telecommunication and Telecontrol

655 Graphic Industries. Printing

656 Transport and Postal Services

657 Accountancy

658 Business Management

659 Publicity, Public Relations.

Management aspect of all the services is dealt by this class. The related engineering aspects are dealt under 62 Engineering class. 654 is Telecommunication Services management whereas 621.39 is Telecommunication engineering. 656 Transport services whereas Transport (Vehicle) engineering is 629.

While individual subjects are treated under the relevant classses, compound subjects where both the aspects are to be represented, colon is used to combine the numbers from both the classes. For example Transmission of messages by fax machine is given a number 654.17:621.397.12. Here transmission of messages is a transport service and hence the number 654.17 and fax machine is a device in Telecommunication engineering and so 621.397.12.

Special common auxiliaries .0 are used under each class to represent different concepts. 654.02 Telecommunication routes, lines., 655.02 Working Processes, 656.02 Transport routes, services. However, special auxiliaries .0 listed at 65 are applicable to 658 without any modifications.

Social sciences classes are related to Management class. Hence colon is to be used to combine numbers from these two classes.

66 Chemical technology and related industries. Applied Chemistry is included here. Materials based on chemical processes are included in this class, while composition of chemical compounds is included in 54. All technologies such as Fuels, Food, Oil, Glass, Ceramics, Paints and Metallurgy are included in this class. Special auxiliary subdivisions .0 are provided at 66 to represent chemical processes and these are common to all technologies.

Detailed concepts may be expressed through synthesis by

using both colon and special auxiliary subdivision :0 and in Metallurgy class - is used to express state of the metals or alloys. These auxiliaries are taken from 62-1/-9. Special common auxiliary ' is also used to express alloys (combination of metals).

Like 62 class for Engineering, 66 class for technology is also very exhaustive and is considered to be the mainstay of the UDC.

67 Various industries, trades and crafts. This class is for industries based on technologies of 66 class manufacture and trade. Industries based on precious metals, ferrous, non ferrous metals, leather, timber and wood work, pulp and paper, textiles, rubber and plastics, wires, stones etc are included in this class.

68 Industries, crafts and trades for finished or assembled articles.This class is also a continuation of 66 and 67 but devoted to finished products based on the 66 and 67 classes. The class starts with 681 Precision mechanisms and instruments where instrumentation and computers are the major classes with 681.2 and 681.3 respectively are the class numbers. Other Precision mechanisms and instruments are covered in 681.4 to 681.9. Trades like smithery, iron mongery, furniture making, upholstery, foot wear, bookbinding, garment industry, toys and handicrafts are covered by 682/689.

69 class is allotted to Building trade : Construction material , Building practices. The class subdivisions are 691 Building materials. 692 Structural parts of buildings 693 Masonry 694 Timber 696 Services and installations in buildings. 697 Heating, Ventilating and airconditioning of buildings 698 Finishing and decorating trades. 699 Protection of buildings. Special auxiliary subdivision .0 are used for common concepts.

3.6 CLASS 7 ARTS, RECREATION, ENTERTAINMENT, SPORT

Covers modern arts, fine arts and subdivisions include 71 Physical planning 72 Architecture 73 Plastic Arts 74 Technical drawing, Design, Applied Arts and crafts which are subdivided as 741 Drawing 742 Perspective in drawing 743 Anatomical drawing 744 Technical drawing 745 Decorative handicrafts 746

Fancy work 747 Interior decoration 748 Vitreous Arts, Glass and crystal ware. 749 Artistic furniture 75 Painting 76 Graphics 77 Photography 78 Music 79 Recreation, Entertainment and Sports.

Most of the subdivisions in this class are related to the earlier classes so far as the subjects are concerned. However the treatment of subjects is different in each class. 72 Architecture is related to 69 Building industry. 77 Photography is related to 66 Chemical technology. 771 Equipment connected with Optics is related to 535.31 Lenses and other equipment. 785 Music for instruments is related to 681.8 Musical instruments. One will find many such examples.

3.7 CLASS 8. LANGUAGE, LINGUISTICS. LITERATURE

Covers both language and literature. In the earlier editions of the UDC, 4 was allotted to Language and 8 to Literature. Now class 4 is vacant and 8 class includes language and literature.

Classes 80 and 81 are allotted to Language and Linguistics and 82 is for Literature. In fact 80 class is for general aspects of language and literature. Philology and 81 is for language and linguistics.

Special auxiliary subdivisions -11/-26 and '1/'443 are used at 81 to be applicable throughout 81 and 811. These subdivisions are used to represent linguistic aspects of particular language or language groups.

Common auxiliary division of Languages =1/=9 are used at 811 to derive individual languages from the Language tables(table 1c).

In case of 82 Literature, special auxiliary subdivisions -1/ -9 are used to represent various forms of literature. .0 subdivisions are used for theory, study and technique of literature. 'subdivisions are used for origin and periods of languages. Phases of development. Individual literatures are derived from Language table 1c. However, a point is to be substituted for equals sign.

3.8 CLASS 9. GEOGRAPHY. BIOGRAPHY. HISTORY

This class is wholly dependent on common auxiliaries of Place and common auxiliaries of Time as the subject geography means place and time only.

Special auxiliary subdivisions - and .0 are extensively used to synthesize the subjects. One would also notice that the schedules of Geography do not occupy many pages when compared to the classes so far dealt with. Here analysis and synthesis is required to represent subjects and for that process the other classes are used alongwith Geography. Hence subdivisions are not enumerated. Special auxiliary subdivisions ' are also used for types of culture.

Geography and history of various countries are classified according to common auxiliaries of Place and Time.

4

Classification Process

Universal Decimal Classification is a versatile classification scheme. Its importance lies in its simple and pure notation. It is easily comprehendable. It is a lucidly understandable artificial language to represent natural language. It is an enumerative scheme and as such a layman can easily follow the notation for all practical purposes. With the help of multi faceted auxiliary apparatus, complex and compound subjects can be analysed, synthesised and represented fully to its exact depth. Index also plays a very important role in knowing the subjects in their proper perspective. A separate index volume is provided along with the main tables which is an indication that the index is very exhaustive in nature. From the index itself, the numbers can be adopted and assigned. This makes classification process faster. This will eliminate the delay in the classification of documents which normally is the case with other classification schemes.

4.1 CLASSIFICATION PROCESS : STEP BY STEP

Step 1: Scan the title of the document to be classified and select important keywords from the title.

Step 2: Refer the index for each keyword and note the main subjects from the notation given in the index against the keyword.

Step 3:Identify the keywords with the main subjects in relation to the contents of the book.

Step 4: Go to the main class that is predominant in the contents of the book.

Step 5: Go through the subdivisions under the above main class as per the notation taken from the index.

Step 6:Fix the total number i.e.,Main class and subdivisions. This forms the first part of the number to be assigned to the document.

Step 7: See the other subjects, if any, that are covered by the document.

Step 8: Go to the index and again note down the subjects with their notation.

Step 9:Go to the class with the notation and repeat the exercise of identifying main class and its subdivisions.

Step10: Coin the number with main class and its subdivisions. This forms second part of the number to be assigned to the document.

Step 11: Identify the nature of relation between the Primary number(class) and secondary number(class).

Step 12: Select the common auxiliary relevant to the relation identified above.

Step 13: Combine the primary and secondary numbers with the common auxiliary.

Step14: See any other common auxiliary is required for the contents to be represented. Identify the same.

Step15: Combine the above common auxiliary to the number derived at Step 13.

Step 16: Form the final number if no other common auxiliaries and special auxiliaries are required.

4.2 CLASSIFICATION PROCESS : SCHEMATIC

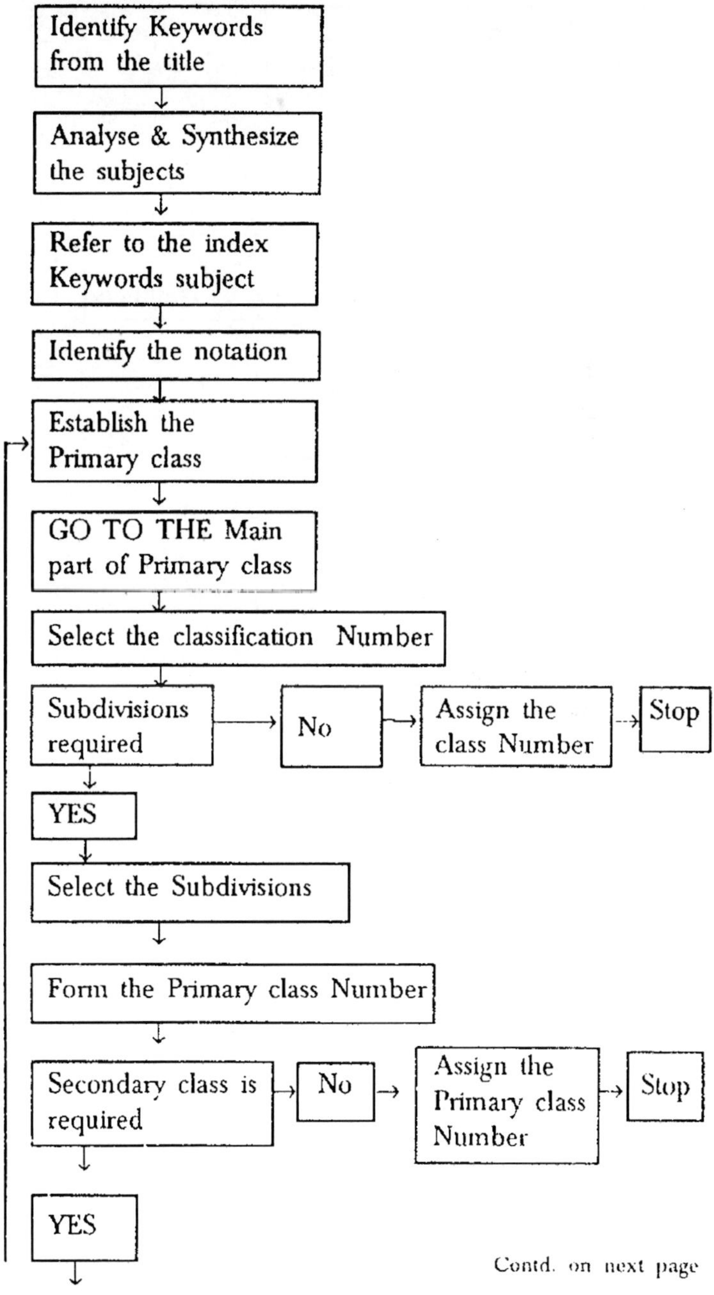

Contd. on next page

Contd. from last page

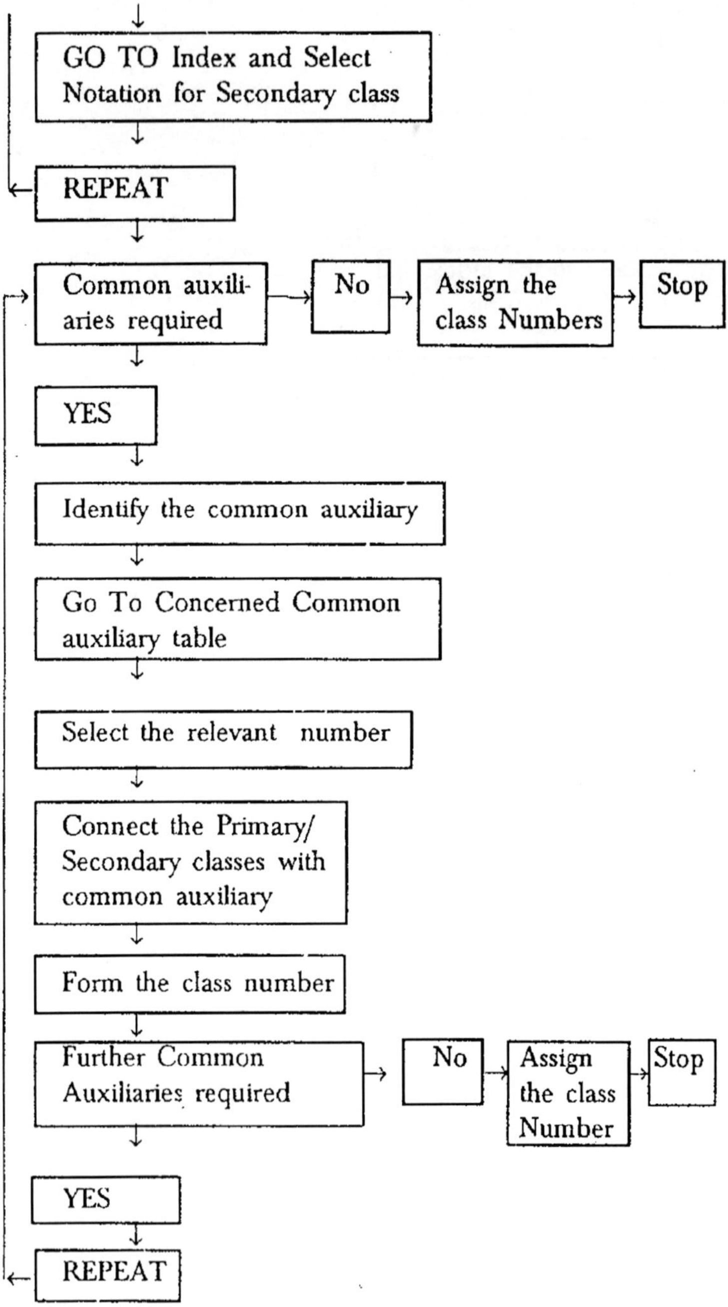

5

Classification Problems : Worked Out Solutions

We have gone through the various features of the Universal Decimal classification scheme. Now we shall work out some problems to give a practical impetus to the use of this classification scheme.

The examples included in this chapter are expected to represent each class with its subdivisions. The examples are so selected that they take care of the use of common auxiliaries, special auxiliaries, various symbols and signs and other features that are unique to the UDC. Some 200 worked out problems are illustrated for the benefit of users of the UDC in various planes. Simple, compound and complex numbers are chosen to benefit the users while doing classification work and to impart practical knowledge in the use of the UDC for both the practitioner and to the layman alike. All the solutions have been thoroughly illustrated in a lucid manner so that the user will immediately grasp the knowledge for the use of the UDC.

5.0 0. GENERALIA

Problem 1:

Encyclopedia of Associations in UK.

Key words : Associations
Encyclopedia
UK (Place)

Look up to Index: Associations 06

Associations general is given 06. Association concerned with specific subjects are given subject classes. Since we are concerned with Associations in general, we have to take 06 number.

Primary number is 06.

Any subdivisions required ? No.

We come to next keyword. Encyclopedia. we go to index again to search for Encyclopedia. Encyclopedias Id (031), 030.

Here two numbers represent table Id: Common auxiliaries of Form and Generalia class 030.

In this particular example encyclopedia is treated as a form and not as a main class. Hence we have to select (031). As explained under table Id, Form common auxiliary should be used with the sign (0..). Accordingly encyclopedia form is (031).

Look for index UK. United Kingdom Ie (410). United Kingdom is treated as place. We have to select from the table Ie common auxiliary of Place. Common auxiliary Place is used with the sign (1/9..). So United Kingdom is (410).

We have found numbers for the three keywords

Associations	06
Encyclopedia	(031)
United Kingdom	(410)

This title has a simple number with auxiliaries of Form and Place. According to the citation order for various auxiliaries: the auxiliaries of Form takes precedence over the Place auxiliaries. Therefore the classification number to the title: Encyclopedia of Associations in UK is *06(031)(410).*

Problem 2:

Thesaurus of Engineering and scientific terms.

Key words: Thesaurus
Engineering
Science.

Look up Index: Thesaurii: 025.4.05,025.4.06,025.43

025.4.05 Indexing and retrieval languages for the whole of knowledge.

025.4.06 Indexing and retrieval languages for special subjects. Special thesaurus.

025.43 Controlled term lists. Thesaurii. Descriptor lists.

Here the title is about controlled term lists and not for indexing and retrieval languages. Hence 025.43 is the relevant notation. Thesaurus 025.43.

This title is a compound title and requires more than one main class. We have to look up to index for the classes: Engineering and Sciences.

Engineering : 6

Sciences : 5

The two classes have consecutive numbers in the schedules. Both the subjects are included in totality. Hence we have to use the connecting symbol '/' to connect two consecutive numbers. The order is science and Engineering in the schedules. Therefore, it is customary to follow citation order as per the schedules although the title here is in reverse order. Hence the number here is 5/6. The title refers to two(three) classes. They are related also. Thesaurus is related to engineering and science. Hence to combine the two classes the relation sign : is used. Accordingly

Thesaurus : Engineering/Science

025.43 : 5/6

Any common auxiliaries required ? No.

025.43:5/6 Thesaurus of Engineering and Scientific terms.

(Note: Here two relational signs are used : and /)

Problem 3:

Reference service in University Libraries in India.

Keywords : Reference Service
Libraries - University
India (Place)

Main class : Librarianship : 02

Subclass : Libraries - General : 027

Subdivision Libraries of institutions of higher education. Including University Libraries. 027.7

Subdivision : Reference Service 025.5
Place common auxiliary : India (540)

Here a compound subclass is existing. University Libraries and Reference Services. These two are related in this particular title although they are independent. Hence a classifier has to keep his users' interest in mind and decide on to which subclass should be given prominence over the other subclass. Therefore, it is possible to classify this document in more than one way thus:

Libraries - University Libraries - Reference Service India.
02 - 027.7 - 025.5 - (540)

or 027.7 : 025.5 (540)

Since this is a compound subject (title) relation sign : is used. It may be noted that : is used within the same main class i.e. 02 Librarianship to represent two independent subclasses 027.7 and 025.5. Alternatively, we can change the sequence of the notation by giving priority to Reference service instead of University libraries as above. It would be

025:027.7(540) Reference service in University Libraries in India

One may feel that the important concepts are missing if the book is classified under any one of the above numbers. To obviate such a difficulty, it is recommended that the classified index in the library catalogue be provided with two filing sequences for this title.

This point has been discussed under the section: Multiple entry in the classified file.

Problem 4:

Principles of Artificial Intelligence.

Keyword : Artificial Intelligence.

Index : Artificial Intelligence (cybernetics) 007.52.

Any common auxiliaries required? No.

007.52 Principles of Artificial Intelligence.

Problem 5:

British Books in Print (Trade catalogue of books published by various publishers)

Keywords : Book trade catalogues
Great Britain

Index : Book sellers catalogues 017.41, 018.4,019.4.

Common auxiliary Place: Great Britain (410)

Three numbers are provided for Book sellers catalogue in the index. Here we have to select the general catalogue as collective trade catalogue 017.41 whereas 018.4 and 019.4 are for alphabetical and dictionary catalogues respectively. These two numbers refer to the arrangement of entries in the catalogue.

Catalogues - Book trade catalogues - Great Britain.

Main class : Catalogues 01

Subclass : Catalogues in general 017

Subdivision : Commercial, trade Catalogues 017.4

Subdivision : Collective trade Catalogues 017.41

Common auxiliary Place : Great Britain (410)

017.41(410) British Books in Print.

Problem 6:

Indian National Bibliography.

Keywords : Bibliographies - National India.

Index : Bibliographies 01
National bibliographies 015
India (540)

Main class : Bibliographies 01

Subclass : Bibliographies of Place including National Bibliographies 015

Common auxiliary Place :India (540)

Bibliographies -	National bibliographies -	India
01	015	(540)

015(540) Indian National Bibliography.

Problem 7:

Childrens' encyclopaedia of knowledge.

Keywords : Encyclopaedia
Children.

Main class : General reference works including Encyclopaedias, dictionaries. 031

Special auxiliary
Subdivisions : Children documents 0.053.2

Here 0 = 031.

031.053.2 Childrens' encyclopaedia of knowledge

(Note: Under the main class 030, it is mentioned that the subdivisions are to be taken from common auxiliaries Form (03). Here the subdivisions of (03) and its special auxiliary subdivisions are applicable).

Problem 8:

Use of reports literature.

Keyword : Reports

Main class : Non Serial separates. 04

Subclass : Reports. Notices. Bulletins. 047

Non serial separates - Reports.

047 is the class number for the title 'Use of reports literature'.

Problem 9

Trade reports of France in 20th century.

Keywords : Trade reports

France

20th century.

Main class : Non Serial separates. 04

Sub class : Reports. Notices. Bulletins. 047

Subdivision : Trade reports. Marketing reports. 047.36

Common auxiliary Place : France (44)

" " Time : "19"

Index : Trade reports Id (047.36)

(Note: Trade reports word is indexed under Table Id (047.36) as a form common auxiliary. It is also to be noted that all classes of Generalia are dependent on common auxiliary Form tables wherever otherwise specified).

Reports - Trade reports - France - 20th Century.

047.36(44)"19" Trade reports of France in 20th Century.

Problem 10:

Directory of Periodicals published from USA.

Keywords : Periodicals

Directory

USA

Main class : Periodicals

Common Auxiliary Form : Directory

" " Place : USA

Index

Periodicals : Id (051), 050, 82-92.

Directories : Id (058), 050.8

USA : Ie (73)

Periodicals appear both in Generalia class as main class and in the common auxiliaries of Form table 1e and in Literature as literary form.

In this title the class number for periodicals should be selected from Generalia class as the treatment is general. Therefore, 050 is the relevant Class Number.

In case of directories, the form is important and not the directory itself. Hence the number for the directory should be selected from Table Id Common auxiliaries : form i.e. (058) Place is from table Ie. USA (73).

The required Class Number is *050(058)(73).*

Problem 11

Index to conference proceedings 1974 - 1990 Published by British Library Document Supply Centre 1992.

Keywords : Conferences
Proceedings
Indexes
Period 1974 - 90.

Main class : Organisations and other types of cooperation. 06

Subclass : Societies. Associations. Congresses... 061

Subdivision : Meetings, Symposia, Conferences... 061.3

Special auxiliary Subdivisions : Publications, reports concerning work 06.055

Collections of Printed work: Proceedings, Transactions 06.055.2.

Common auxiliaries of Form : Index of names, Places, Subjects (083.86)

" " Time : "1974 - 90".

(Note: It is assumed that the user will consult the index to arrive at the above main and subclasses with their corresponding class numbers if he is not familiar with the main classes and subclasses)

The citation order for this title is

Conferences - Proceedings - Indexes - Period
061.3 06.055.2 (083.86) "1974/1990"

061.3.055.2(083.86)"1974/1990" is the required class number

Problem 12

Press in India

Keywords : Press

: Newspapers

: India.

Main class : Press. Newspapers. 070

Common auxiliary Place : India (540)

Press/Newspapers - India

070 (540)

070(540) Press in India.

Problem 13

Editing and Design. 5 volumes.

(Newspapers)

Keywords : News Papers

Editing

Design.

Main class : News Papers. 070

Subclass : Editing Practices 070.41

(including design)

News Papers - Editing and Design

070 070.41

The required number is *070.41*

Problem 14

Collections of Juvenile literature. Collective works

Keywords : Children books

Juvenile literature

Telugu.

Main class : Collective works 08

Subclass : Documents of particular origin 087

Subdivision : Publications for young people including juvenile literature 087.5

Collective works - Children's literature - Juvenile literature

087.5 is the required number for the title 'Collections of juvenile literature'.

Problem 15

Collection of Maps of North India.

Keywords : Collective works
Maps
India, North.

Main class : Collective works 08

Subclass : Maps 084

Common auxiliaries of Place : India

Subdivision : North India.

The order should be collective works - Maps - India-North India

08 084 (540) (545)

084(545) is the required number.

Problem 16

Catalogue of out of Print books.

Keywords : Out of Print Books
Directories.

Main class : Manuscripts : Rare and remarkable works 09

Subclass : Other kinds of works, remarkable for extrinsic characteristics 099

Subdivision : Books not in the market. Out of Print editions. 099.4.

Common auxiliaries of form : Catalogues (017)

Rare Books - Out of print books - Catalogues.

0 099.4 (017)

099.4(017) is the required number for the title Catalogue of out of print books.

Problem 17

Manuscripts on papyrus in the 16th century

Keywords : Manuscripts
Papyrus
16th century.

Main class : Manuscripts 091

Subclass : Manuscripts according to writing surface 091.2

Common auxiliaries of Time : 16th century "15"

091.2"15" is the required number for Manuscripts on papyrus in the 16th century.

Problem 18

Indian National Scientific Documentation Centre (INSDOC).

Keywords : Documentation Centres
National Centres
Science
India.

Primary Main class : Documentation 002

Subclass : Documentation Centres

Subdivision : National Documentation Centres 002.63

Secondary Main class : Science

Common auxiliaries of Place : India.

Documentation - Documentation Centres - National
002.6
Documentation Centres - Science - India.
002 - 002.63 5 (540)

Here a relation exists between primary Main class and secondary Main class in this compound subject. Documentation and Science are the two main classes. Relation sign is used to connect them. Therefore the number is

002.63:5 for Science National Documentation Centres.

002.63:5(540) Indian National Scientific Documentation Centre.

Problem 19

Bibliography of festschrifts.

Keywords : Festschrift
Bibliography

Main class : Festschrift 082.2

Common auxiliaries Form : Bibliography (01)

Index : Festschriften 082.2.
Bibliographies Id (01)

The order is Festschrifts - Bibliography

082.2 (01)

The required number is *082.2 (01)* for the title Bibliography of Festschrifts.

Problem 20

Bibliography of bibliographies.

Keyword : Bibliography

Main class : Bibliographies 011

Common auxiliaries of Form : Bibliography (01)

Here the title is some what confusing. It is to be understood that this document is a compilation of various bibliographies published. Hence the subject of the document is bibliographies and the form in which this list is presented is a bibliography.

The required number, therefore, is *011(01)* for the title Bibliography of bibliographies.

5.1 1. PSYCHOLOGY. PHILOSOPHY

Problem 21

Mental disorders in adults of Anglo Saxon races.

Keywords	: Mental disorders
	Adults
	Anglo saxon race.
Main class	: Philosophy. Psychology 1
SubClass	: Psychology 159.9
Subdivision	: Abnormal Psychology 159.97
Subdivision	: Mental disorders. 159.972
Common auxiliaries of Persons	: Adults - 053.8
	Race
(Nationality)	: Anglo Saxon race(=1.410)
Index	: Mental disorders 159.972 (=1.410)
	Adults Ik - 053.8
	Anglo Saxon race. (=1.410)

No entry for Anglo Saxon race. But it can be inferred from the number 942.01 Anglo Saxon Period (Great Britain) that Anglo Saxon is Great Britain. So we can derive a number from the table If. Common auxiliaries of Nationality. (=1.4/.9) Particular nationalities of the modern world.

(=1.4/.9) ≡ (4/9) (Table le)

Great Britain is (410)

Accordingly

(=1.410) is Anglo Saxon race.

The citation order is

Psychology -	Mental disorders -	Adults -	Anglo Saxon race
159.9	159.972	053.8	(=1.410)

The required number is

159.972 - 053.8 (=1.410)

Problem 22

Theory of Cosmogony

Keywords : Cosmogony

Main class : Philosophy 1

Subclass : Metaphysics 11

Subdivision : Cosmogony 113

Any common auxiliaries required? No.

Cosmogony *113*

Problem 23

The search after Truth & Elucidations of search after truth.

Keyword : Truth

Main class : Philosophy 1

Subclass : Metaphysics 11

Subdivision : Truth 111.83

Under the word Truth in Index a number of entries are provided in relation to various subjects. Here we have to go by the subject Metaphysics as described in the book. Hence the number to be selected is 111.83 for Truth.

The required number is *111.83.*

Problem 24

Philosophy & the young child

Key words : Philosophy
Children.

Main class : Philosophy 1
Common auxiliaries of Persons
: Children - 053.2

Philosophy - Young Child (Children)
1 053.2

The required number is *1-053.2.*

Problem 25

Creative ideas and creativity.

Keywords : Creative ideas

Creativity

Index Creative ideas (Teleology) 124.4

Creativity (Education) 37.036.

Here Creativity is a general phenomenon existing in nature. Hence creative ideas can be taken as creativity. Second term creativity (Education) refers to the creativity in Education only.

Main class : Philosophy 1

Subclass : Teleology 124

Subdivision : Creative idea 124.4.

The required number is *124.4*

Problem 26

An inquiry into the Human mind.

Keywords : Mind

Human beings

Philosophy

Index : Mind

Metaphysics 111.7

Philosophy 13

Psychology 159.9.016.1

Main class : Philosophy 13

Subclass : Nature of Mind and Spirit 130.11

The required Number is *130.11*

Problem 27

Astrological Magazine of 1993.

Keywords : Astrology

Magazines

Periodicals

1993.

Main class : Philosophy 1

Subclass : Philosophy of Mind and Spirit

Subdivision : 133.52

Common auxiliaries of Form: Magazines Periodicals (051)

Common auxiliaries of Time : "1993"

Philosophy - Astrology - Magazines - 1993.

1 133.52 (051) "1993"

Astrological Magazine of 1993 *133.52 (051) "1993"*

Problem 28

Theism and Philosophy.

Keywords : Theism
Philosophy.

Main class : Philosophy 1

Subclass : Philosophical points of view 14

Subdivision : Kinds of view point 141

Sub subdivision: Theism 141.41

The Required Number is *141.41*

Problem 29

Marxist Philosophy.

Keywords : Marxism
Philosophy.

Main class : Philosophy 1

Subclass : Kinds of view point 141

Subdivision : Socialistic Schools and Systems 141.8

Sub subdivision : Scientific Socialism. Marxism 141.82

Philosophy - Marxism

1 141.82

141.82 is the required number.

Problem 30

Behavioural Psychology.

Keywords : Psychology
Behaviour

Index : Behaviour
Psychology 159.9.019.4

The citation order

Psychology - Behaviour

159.9 159.9.019.4

Main class : Psychology.159.9

Special auxiliary Subdivisions : Reaction Psychology. Behaviour

159.9.019.4

159.9.019.4 Behaviour Psychology.

Problem 31

Lateral thinking.

Keywords : Thinking

Index : Thinking.
Psychology 159.955

Main class : Psychology 159.9

Subclass : Higher Mental Processes

Subdivision : Thinking. Thought 159.955

159.955 Lateral thinking

Problem 32

Behavioural Psychology of abnormal children.

Keywords : Psychology
- Behaviour
Children
- abnormal.

Index : Behaviour 159.9.019.4
Child Psychology 159.922.7

Abnormal children is listed under 159.922.76

Main class : Psychology 159.9

Subclass : Child Psychology 159.922.7

Subdivision : Abnormal children 159.922.76

Special auxiliary

Subdivision : Behaviour 159.9.019.4

Psychology -	Child Psychology -	Abnormal children -	Behaviour
159.9	159.922.7	159.922.76	.019.4.

The required number is *159.922.76.019.4*

Problem 33

Theory of reasoning in Natural Sciences.

Keywords : Reasoning
Natural Sciences
Logic

Primary Main class : Logic 16

Subclass : Reasoning 162

Secondary Main class : 5

Compound Subject : Reasoning related to Natural Sciences

162:5 is the required number.

Problem 34

Principles of Epistemology.

Keyword : Epistemology

Main class : Logic 16

Subclass : Epistemology 165

165 Principles of Epistemology

Problem 35

Cognitive paradigms in knowledge organisation.

Keywords : Cognition
Knowledge
Organization

Index Cognition (theory of knowledge) 165.171

Cognitive knowledge 165.194

Knowledge 001

Organisation 001.89.

Primary Main
class : Logic 16
Subclass : Theory of knowledge 165
Subdivision : Cognitive knowledge 165.194
Secondary Main
class : Knowledge 001
Subclass : Organisation of Scientific work 001.89.
Relation : Cognitive knowledge
: Knowledge organisation.

Therefore the required number is *165.194:001.89.*

Problem 36

War and Peace (International ethics)

The title represents the subject of relations among nations.

Main subject is Social ethics.

Ethics : 17
Social Ethics : 172

Relation between Nations (Moral) = 172.4

Under 172.4 is listed War and Peace. International Ethics.

172.4 is the number for War and Peace

Problem 37

Family life in India during 20th Century.

Keywords : Family ethics
Family life
India
20th Century
Main class : Ethics 17
Subclass : Family ethics 173
Subdivision : Family life 173.7
Common auxiliaries
of Place : India (540)

Common auxiliaries
of Time : "19"

Ethics - Family ethics - Family life - India - Time
17 173 173.7 (540) "19"

The required number is *173.7(540)"19"*

Problem 38

Occupational ethics	:	Theory and Practice.
Main class	:	Ethics 17
Occupational ethics	:	174
Index	:	Occupational ethics 174.

174 is Occupational ethics.

Problem 39

Morals of dancing.

Keywords	:	Ethics Morals - recreation. Dancing.
Primary Main Class	:	Ethics 17
Subclass	:	Ethics of recreation 175
Secondary Main Class	:	Arts 7
Subclass	:	Social entertainment 793
Subdivision	:	Dances 793.3.

The required number is *175:793.3.*

Problem 40

Search for Society	:	Biosocial science and morality.
Keywords	:	Social ethics Morals.
Main class	:	Ethics. Morals. 17
Subclass	:	Social ethics. 172

Special auxiliary subdivisions : Nature of the morals .02
172.02 is the required number.

5.2 **2. RELIGION**

Problem 41

God beyond religion : Personal journeying from religiousity to spirituality.

Key words	: God
	: Religion
	Spiritualism
Primary Main Class	: Religion 2
Subclass	: Theology 21
Subdivision	: God 211
Secondary Main Class	: Philosophy 1
Subclass	: Philosophical System 14
Subdivision	: Spiritualism 141.135
	Religion - God -Spiritualism.

211:141.35 God beyond Religion.

Problem 42

Selected Writings on Religion and Society.

Keywords	: Religion
	Society
Primary Main Class	: Religion 2
Secondary Main Class	: Society. Social ethics 172.3

2:172.3 Religion and Society.

Problem 43

Creative scepticism in seventeenth century England

Keywords	: Creativity
	Scepticism
	17th Century
	England.
Primary Main Class	: Religion 2
Subclass	: Natural theology 21
Subdivision	: Scepticism 211.5
Secondary Main Class	: Philosophy 1
Subclass	: Creativity 124.4
Common auxiliaries of Place	: England (410.1)
Common auxiliaries of Time	: Seventeenth century"16"

The citation order :

Religion - Scepticism - Creative idea - England - 17th Century

2 211.5 124.4 (410.1) "16"

211.5:124.4(410.1)"16" is the required number.

Problem 44

Bible in German.

Keywords : Bible
German language.

Index : Bible 22
German language lc = 112.2

Main class : Religion 2

Subclass : The Bible. Holy Scripture 22

Common auxiliaries Language : German = 122.2

Religion - The Bible - in German

2 22 = 112.2

22=112.2 The Bible in German.

Problem 45

Commentaries on the New testament.

Keywords : Bible
New testament
Commentaries.

Main class : Religion 2

Subclass : Bible 22

Subclass : New Testament 225.

Special auxiliary
subdivisions : Commentaries .07

Religion - Bible - New Testament - Commentaries

2 22 225 .07

225.07 Commentaries on New Testament.

Problem 46

The reappearance of the Christ.

Keywords : Christ
Main class : Religion 2
Subclass : Christianity 23/28
Subclass : Last things. Eschatology 236
Subdivision : Second coming of Christ 236.93

236.93 Reappearance of the Christ.

Problem 47

Catechism of modern man.

Keyword : Catechism
Main class : Religion 2
Subclass : Dogmatic theology 23
Subsubclass : Symbols of faith 238
Subdivision : Catechisms 238.1

238.1 Catechism of modern man.

Problem 48

Understanding Sunday School Books.

Keywords : Sunday Schools Books
Index : Sunday Schools- Books 244

Religion - Practical theology - Religious literature
2 24 244

244 Understanding Sunday School Books.

Problem 49

Polity and Praxis : A Programme for American Practical theology.

Keywords : Theology - Practical
America.
Main class : Religion 2
Subclass : Theology, Practical 24
Common auxiliaries
of Place : America (73)

Religion - Practical theology - America.
2 24 (73)

24(73) American Practical theology.

Problem 50

Christian Preachings : Religious Sermons

Keywords	:	Christianity Preachings Sermons
Main class	:	Religion 2
Subclass	:	Christianity 23/28
Subclass	:	Pastoral theology 25
Subdivision	:	Preachings 251
Subdivision	:	Sermons 252.

Religion-Christianity - Pastoral theology - Preachings-
2 23/28 25 251
Sermons
252

251/252 Christian Preachings - Religious Sermons.

(Note : Preachings and Sermons are classified under 251 and 252 respectively. We require both the classes and since they are consecutive classes we can use / extension sign. Hence 251/252)

Problem 51

Vocational training in priesthood in South Africa.

Keywords	:	Priesthood Training - Vocational South Africa.
Main class	:	Religion 2
Subclass	:	Pastoral theology 25
Sub subclass	:	Priesthood 254
Subdivision	:	Education and training 254.4
Sub subdivision	:	Vocation 254.41
Common auxiliaries of Space	:	South Africa (680)
Citation order	:	

Religion-Christianity-Theology,Pastoral- Priesthood-
2 23/28 25 254
Education and Training-Vocation- South Africa
254.4 254.41 (680)

254.41(680) Vocational training in priesthood in South Africa.

Problem 52

16th Century Churches of South India

Keywords : Churches
South India
16th Century

Main class : Religion 2

Subclass : Christian Churches 28

Subdivision : Non Roman Catholic churches 283

Common auxiliaries of Place : South India (548)

Common auxiliaries of Time : 16th Century "15".

Religion-Christian Churches-Non Roman Catholic Churches-
2 28 283
South India- 16th Century.
(548) "15"

283(548)"15" 16th century Churches of South India.

Problem 53

Soviet studies on the church and the believers response to atheism.

Keywords : Churches
: Atheism
: Faith

Main class : Religion 2

Primary Subclass . Christianity 23/28

Subdivision : Churches 26

Secondary Subclass : Natural theology 21

Subdivision : Atheism 211.5

Tertiary Subclass : Practical theology 24
Subdivision : Faith 241.511

Religion - Christianity - Churches
I 2 23/28 26

Religion - Natural theology - Atheism
II 2 21 211.5

Religion - Practical theology - Faith
III 2 24 241.511

26:211.5:241.511 Soviet Studies on the church and the believers response to atheism.

(Note: Here is a typical example of three subclasses in the same main class related to one another).

Problem 54

Christian Missionaries in Kerala, India.

Keywords : Christianity
Missionaries
Kerala, India.

Main class : Religion 2
Subclass : Christianity 23/28
Christian Church 26
Subdivision : Priests and Clerics in general. Various clerical offices 262.14
Sub division : Missionaries 262.146
Common auxiliaries of Place : Kerala (548.3)

Religion - Christianity - Christian Churches - Church offices -
2 23/28 26 262.14

Missionaries - Kerala,India.
262.146 (548.4)

262.146(548.4) Christian missionaries in Kerala, India.

Problem 55

Understanding Sunday Schools.

Keywords : Sunday Schools

Main class : Religion 2

Subclass : Christian Churches 26

Subclass : Sunday Schools 268

Religion - Christian Churches - Sunday Schools

2 26 268

268 Understanding Sunday Schools.

(Please also see problem 48)

Problem 56

Religious institutes, Secular institutes, Societies of the Apostolic life.

Keywords : Religion.
- Institutes
Apostolics
-Societies.

Main class : Religion 2

Primary Subclass : Religious Assns. Societies 267

Subdivision : Apostolic Succession 262.11

Religion - Christian Church - Religious Assns - Apostolic succession.

2 26 267 262.11

267:262.11 is the required number.

Alternately the class at Associations can be considered:
061.234 (06 Associations
061 Organisations, Institutions
061.2 Private organisations
061.23 Organisations with special purpose
061.234 Religious Institutes)

Apostolic Succession of Religious Associations is
061.234:262.11

Thus the above title can be placed under two main classes 2 and 0 depending on the requirement of the individual library.

Problem 57

Upanishads in Telugu.

Keywords	: Upanishads (Hindu Sacred works)
	: Telugu
Main class	: Religion 2
Subclass	: Non Christian Religion 29
Subclass	: Hindu Religion 294
Subdivision	: Vedism 294.11
Subdivision	: Sacred books Upanishads 294.118

Common auxiliaries of Language : Telugu = 572.24

Under 294.11 Vedism an instruction appears thus 294.11 ≡ 291. ≡ indicates the division of left side number as per the right side number to this symbol ≡. Here right side number is 291 and the division of 291 to 291.8 is for sacred books. Since Upanishads are sacred books of Vedism the number 294.11 is divided to represent Upanishads as 294.118 (294.11 = 291 and therefore 291.8 = 294.118).

Accordingly, Upanishads 294.118

Telugu language = 572.24.

Therefore, Upanishads in Telugu is notationally represented as *294.118=572.24*

Problem 58

Influence of Buddhism on Hinduism.

Keywords	: Buddhism
	Hinduism
Main class	: Religion 2
Subclass	: Non Christian Religions 29
Sub subclass	: Religion of the Hindus 294
Primary Subdivision	: Buddhism 294.3
Secondary Subdivision	: Hinduism 294.5

Religion-NonChristianReligion-Religion of Hindus-Buddhism-
2 29 294 294.3

Hinduism Influence relation
294.5

Here an Influence relation exists between Buddhism and Hinduism. We have to use relation sign: Accordingly, *294.3:294.5* is the required number.

(Note: The relation is within the same subclass).

Problem 59

A study of the administration of Hindu Public Religious trusts in Madras.

Keywords	:	Hinduism
		Religious trusts
		Administration
		Madras
Index	:	Hinduism 294.5
Religious associations	:	061.234.
		Madras State (548.1)
		Capital cities. Madras (548.1-25)

294.5:061.234(548.1-25) is the required number.

Problem 60

Jewish Prayers.

Keyword	:	Jewish Religion Prayers.
Main class	:	Religion 2
Subclass	:	Non Christian Religions 29
Subclass	:	Jewish religion 296.
Subdivision	:	Jewish Prayers 296.3

Religion - Non Christian Religion - Jewish religion - Prayers
2 29 296 296.3

296.3 Jewish Prayers.

5.3 3.SOCIAL SCIENCES

Problem 61

Methods of Social Research

Keywords : Social Sciences
Research Methodology

Main class : Social sciences 3

Subclass : Theories, Methodology 30

Subdivision : Methods of Social Sciences 303

Subdivision : Social Research 303.1

Social Sciences - Theories, Methodology - Methods - Research
3 30 303 303.1

303.1 Methods of Social Research.

Problem 62

Causal models in Social Sciences.

Keywords : Social Sciences
Causal methods

Index : Social Sciences 3
Causal analysis 303.724
Models 303.09

Social Sciences - Methods of Social Sciences - Analysis 3
3 303 303.7

Procedures - Kinds of analysis - Causal analysis - Models
303.72303 724303 724.09

303.724.09 Causal models in Social Sciences.

Problem 63

Introduction to statistics for geographers and earth scientists.

Keywords : Statistics
Geographers
Earth Scientists.

Primary Main class : Social Sciences 3
Subclass : Statistics 31
Secondary Main class : Geography 91
Special auxiliary
subdivision : Geographers. 91-051
Tertiary Main class : Earth sciences 55
Special auxiliary
Subdivision : Earth Scientists 55 - 051

The required number is *31:91-051+55-051* or by using algebraic sub grouping sign [ ] We can make this number to look like *31:[91+55]-051*.

Problem 64

Understanding Sociology through fiction.

Keywords : Sociology
Fiction
Primary Main class : Social Sciences 3
Subclass : Sociology 316
Secondary Main class : Language, Literature 8
Subclass : Literature 82
Special auxiliary
Subdivision : Fiction 82-3

Social Sciences -	Sociology -	Language. Literature -	Literature -
3	316	8	82

Fiction
82-3

316:82-3 Understanding Sociology through fiction.

Problem 65

Indian National Congress : Historical perspective
Keywords : Political Parties
India.
Historical presentation.
Main class : Social Sciences 3

Subclass : Politics 32
Sub subclass : Political parties 329
Common auxiliaries
of Place : India (540)
Alphabetical device : INC
Common auxiliaries
of form : Historical presentation(091)

329(540)INC(091) Indian National Congress Historical perspective.

Problem 66

India's foreign Policy.

Keywords : India
Foreign relations
Foreign Policy
Main class : Social Sciences 3
Subclass : Politics 32
Subdivision : International relations 327
Common auxiliaries
of Place : India (540)

327(540) India's foreign Policy.

Problem 67

Minimum wages Act.

Keywords : Wages
Labour
Acts.
Index : Minimum wages
Labour economics 331.215.53.
Acts.Legal documents (094.5)

Economics -	Labour -	Wages. -	Minimum wages -	Acts
33	331	331.2	331.215.53	(094.5)

—*331.215.53(094.5)* Minimum wages act.

Problem 68

Foreign Exchange Regulation Act (FERA) India.

Keywords : Currency
Foreign Exchange
Regulations
Acts
India

Main class : Social Sciences 3

Subclass : Economics 33

Subclass : Trade. Commerce. World economy 339

Subdivision : Exchange control. 339.746

Common auxiliaries of Form : Acts (094.5)

Common auxiliaries of Place : India (540)

339.746(540)(094.5) is the required number.

Problem 69

A working bibliography of Greek Law.

Keywords : Law
Greek
Bibliographies

Main class : Law 34

Common auxiliaries of Place : Greece (495)

Common auxiliaries of Form : Bibliography (01)

34(495)(01) Bibliography of Greek law.

Problem 70

Of men and not of law : The courts are usurping the political function.

Keywords : Courts
Law
Politics.

Main class : Law 34

Subclass : Courts 342.519

Secondary Main class : 32

342.519:32 is the required number.

Problem 71

Training for Public Administration & Management in Developing countries : A Review

Keywords : Public Administration
Training
Developing Countries

Main class : Social Sciences 3

Subclass : Public Administration 35

Special auxiliary subdivisions : Training 35.088.6

Common auxiliaries of Place : Developing Countries (1-773)

35.088.6(1-773) is the required number.

Problem 72

Limits to Bureaucratic growth.

Keywords : Bureaucracy

There is no word in the index as bureaucracy. We have to infer the meaning for bureaucracy as top level administrative body.

Top level administration has a number 354.

Hence we can adopt *354* for the title : Limits to bureaucratic growth.

Problem 73

Consumer protection in India.

Keywords : Consumerism
Consumer Protection
India.

Main class : Social Sciences 3

Subclass : Social work. Social aid 36

Sub subclass : Consumerism 366

Subdivision : Consumer protection 366.5

Common auxiliaries of Place : India (540)

366.5(540) Consumer protection in India.

Problem 74

Use of Audiovisual methods in primary school education in India.

Keywords : Audio Visual methods
School Education
India.

Primary Main class : Education 37

Subclass : Kinds of Schools 373

Sub subclass : Primary Schools 373.3

Secondary Main class : Teaching methods 371.3

Subclass : Oral instruction 371.33

Subdivision : Audiovisual methods 371.333

Common auxiliaries of Place : India (540)

Education - Primary Schools - Teaching methods -
37 373.3 371.3
Audio visual methods - India.
371.333 (540)

373.3:371.333(540) Use of Audio Visual methods in primary school education in India.

Problem 75

Social regulation : Strategies for reforms

Keywords : Social Control
Social reforms.

Main class : Social Sciences 3

Sub class : Sociology 31
Subdivision : Social Change 316.42
Subdivision : Social Change reform 316.422
316.422 Social regulation : Strategies for reforms.

Problem 76

Professional Education for Social work in Britain : An historical account.

Keywords : Social work
Education
Britain
Historical
Primary Main class : Education 37
Subclass : Special subject education 373.6
Secondary Main class : Social Problems 364
Subclass : Social work. 364.442.2
Common auxiliaries of Place : Britain (410)
Common auxiliaries of form : Historical.

373.6:364.442.2(410)(091) is the required number.

Problem 77

Introduction to Metrology.

Keyword : Metrology
Main class : Social Sciences 3
Subclass : Metrology 389

389 Introduction to Metrology

Problem 78

Units of Measurement : an encyclopaedic dictionary of units.

Keywords : Units
Measurement
Dictionary

Main class : Social Sciences 3
Subclass : Metrology 389
Subdivision : Units of Measurement 389.16
Common auxiliaries
of Form : Dictionary (038)
389.16(038) Units of Measurement : dictionary.

Problem 79

The wonderful world of Superstition, Prophecy and Luck.
Keywords : Superstition
Prophecy.
Main class : Social Sciences 3
Subclass : Ethnology 39
Subdivision : Superstition 398.3.
398.3 The wonderful world of Superstition.

Problem 80

Folk songs of tribals in India.
Keywords : Folk songs
Tribals
India.
Main class : Social Sciences 3
Subclass : Folk Songs 398.8.
Common auxiliaries of Races : (=081)
Common auxiliaries of Place : (540)
398.8(540)(=081) is the required number.

5.4 5. MATHEMATICS. NATURAL SCIENCES

Problem 81

Great Men of Science.
Keywords : Science
Scientists.
Main class : Science 50

Special common auxiliaries : Scientists - 051.

50-051 Great men of Science.

Problem 82

National Remote sensing in India.

Keywords : Remote sensing, India.

Primary Main class : Science 50

Subclass : Environmentology 504

Subclass : Monitoring Systems 504.064.3

Secondary Main class : Science 50

Subclass : Astronomy 52

Subclass : Geodesy. Surveying 528

Subdivision : Remote sensing 528.8.

504.064.3:528.8(540) National Remote sensing in India.

Problem 83

Theory of differential equations : Worked out examples.

Keywords : Mathematical analysis Differential equations. Solutions.

Main class : Sciences 5

Subclass : Mathematics 51

Subclass : Analysis 517

Subdivision : Differential equations 517.9

Common auxiliaries of form : Solutions (076.2)

517.9(076.2) Theory of differential equations worked out examples.

Problem 84

Theory of Error Correcting Codes.

Keywords : Codes. Error correction systems

Main class : Mathematics 51

Subclass : Error correction systems 519.718.

519.718 Theory of Error Correcting Codes.

Problem 85

Calculus of variations.

Keywords : Variational Calculus
Calculus.

Main class : Mathematics 51

Subclass : Analysis 517

Subdivision : Differential equations 517.9

Subdivision : Calculus of variations 517.97

517.97 Calculus of variations.

Problem 86

Origin, formation of the Solar system.

Keywords : Solar System
Origin

Main class : Astronomy 52

Subclass : Solar System 523

Special auxiliary
subdivision : Origin, formation 523-52.

Sciences - Astronomy - Solar Systrm - Origin, formation.

5 52 523 523-52

523-52 Origin, formation of the Solar system.

Problem 87

Gravitational collapse of neutron stars.

Keywords : Neutron stars
Gravitational pull

Main class : Astronomy 52

Subclass : Stars 524

Subdivision : Peculiar Stars 524.35

Subdivision : Neutron Stars 524.354.6.

Special auxiliary
subdivision : Gravitational interaction
52 - 423.

524.354.6-423 Gravitational collapse of neutron stars.

Problem 88

Introduction to Quantum mechanics

Keywords : Quantum theory

Main class : Physics 53

Subclass : Quantum theory 530.145

530.145 Introduction to Quantum mechanics

Problem 89

Flow induced vibrations : Conference proceedings

Keywords : Flow
Vibrations
Proceedings

Primary Main class : Physics 53

Primary Main subclass : Fluid Mechanics 532.5

Secondary subclass : Vibrations 534.01

Common auxiliaries of Form : Proceedings (063)

532.5:534.01(063) Flow induced Vibrations : Proceedings

Problem 90

Cavitational flow : Proceedings of international conference.

Keywords : Flow
Cavitation
Conference proceedings

Main class : Physics 53

Subclass : Fluid Mechanics 532

Subdivision : Cavitation 532.528

Common auxiliaries of Form : Proceedings(063)

532.528(063) is the required number

Problem 91

Measurement of the density of gases using Chemical phenomena.

Keywords : Measurements
Gases - Density
Chemical Phenomenon

Main class : Physics 53

Subclass : Mechanics 531

Subdivision : Measurement of geometric and mechanical quantities 531.7

Subdivision : Measurement of mass and density 531.75

Subdivision : Measurement of density of gases 531.758

Special auxiliary subdivision : Using Chemical Phenomenon .0828

531.758.082.8 Measurement of the density of gases using Chemical Phenomena.

Problem 92

Low speed wind tunnel testing.

Keywords : Wind tunnels
Aerodynamics
Testing

Main class : Physics 53
Aerodynamics 533.6

Special auxiliary subdivision : Wind tunnels 533.6.071

Common auxiliaries Points of view : testing .001.4

533.6.071.001.4 Low speed wind tunnel testing.

Problem 93:

Handbook of noise control

Keywords : Noise control
Handbooks

Index : Noise control
acoustics 534.83
Handbooks (035)

534.83(035) Handbook of noise control

Problem 94:

Introduction to lasers.

Keywords : Lasers
Light amplification

Index : Lasers
Luminiscence 535.374

535.374 Amplification of radiation by stimulated emission (Laser)

535.374 Introduction to lasers

Problem 95

Optical holography : Seminar proceedings

Keywords : Optics
Holography

Here Holography is basically a photography and as such is classified under 778.38. But in this title the technique is used in Optics. Hence the main class for this title should be Physics - Optics.

Primary main class : Physics 53
Subclass : Optics 535
Secondary Main Class : The Arts 7
SubClass : Holography 778.38
Common auxiliaries
Form : Seminar proceedings (063)

535:778.38(063) Optical holography - Proceedings

Problem 96

Numerical solutions of Heat transfer Problems.

Keywords : Heat Transfer
Numerical methods

Main Class : Physics 53
SubClass : Heat 536
Transfer 536.2
Subdivision : Heat *transfer* 536.24
Secondary Main Class : Mathematics 51
SubClass : Numerical Methods 519.61

536.24:519.61 Numerical methods in heat transfer.

Problem 97:

Theory and problems of thermodynamics

Keywords : Thermodynamics
Problems and solutions
Main Class : Physics 53
SubClass : Heat 536
Subdivision : Thermodynamics 536.7
Common auxiliaries of Form : Problems and Solutions (076.2)

536.7(076.2) Theory and problems of thermodynamics

Problem 98:

Introduction to Low temperature Physics.

Keywords : Physics
Low temperature
Main Class : Physics 53
SubClass : Heat 536
Subdivision : Effect of heat input 536.4
Low temperature 536.48

536.48 Low temperature Physics

Problem 99:

Analytical calorimetry

Index : Calorimetry 536.6
Analysis-Chemistry 543

536.6:543 Analytical calorimetry.

Problem 100:

Theory of electromagnetic fields.

Index : Electromagnetics 537.8

537.8 Theory of electromagnetic fields

Problem 101:

High temperature superconductivity

Index : Superconductivity 538.945
High temperature 536.45

538.945:536.45 High temperature superconductivity

Problem 102

Theory of dielectrics

Index : Dielectrics 537.226
Main class : Physics 53
Subclass : Electricity 537
Subdivision : Static Electricity 537.2
Subdivision : Generation 537.22
: Dielectrics 537.226

537.226 Theory of dielectrics

Problem 103

Mercury thermometers for measuring small temperature differences.

Keywords : Thermometer
Measurement
Temperature
Main class : Physics 53
Subclass : Heat 536
Subdivision : Thermometry 536.51
: Mercury Thermometers 536.512
Special auxilary
subdivision : Measurement .08
: Methods of measurement .083
: Measuring small differences .083.62

536.512.083.62 is the required number

Problem 104

High Performance liquid chromatography

Index : Chromatography 543.544
Liquid 543.544.5
High Performance methods 543.068.7

543.544.5.068.7 is the required number.

Problem 105

Industrial electrochemistry

Index : Electrochemistry 544.6
Industrial 621.357

Here the book can be kept under one of the two classes. As mentioned earlier, the class should be decided on the basis of literary warrant, i.e. More number of books available in one class is the class to be given.

544.6 or 621.357 Industrial Electrochemistry.

Problem 106

Theory of atomic absorption spectra.

Index : Atomic absorption spectroscopy 543.421
Main class : Chemistry 54
Subclass : Analytical Chemistry 543
Subclass : Spectral analysis methods 543.4
Subdivision : Atomic absorption Spectra 543.421

543.421 Theory of atomic absorption spectra

Problem 107

Textbook of organic quantitative analysis

Index : Organic Chemistry 547
Quantitative analysis 543.062

547:543.062 is the required number.

Problem 108

Physical Oceanography

Keywords : Oceanography

Index : Oceanography- Physical 551.46

551.46 Physical Oceanography

Problem 109

Estuarian Hydraulics

Keywords : Estuaries
Hydraulics

Main class : Geology 55

Subclass : Hydrology 556

Subdivision : Estuaries 556.54

Subdivision : " Hydraulics 556.546

556.546 Estuarian Hydraulics

Problem 110

Paleozoology of Mammals

Keywords : Mammalia
Paleozoology

Mammals are classified under both Paleontology and Zoology. Here we are concerned with Paleontology aspect of Mammals. Hence we should select

569 for Paleontology of Mammals.

Problem 111

The development of man's skeletal system.

Keywords : Skeletal system
Human body

Main class : Biology 57

Subclass : Human development Anthropology 572

Subdivision : Skeletal system 572.781

Special auxiliary subdivision : Development 57.017.6

572.781.017.6 The development of men's skeletal system.

Problem 112

Molecular Biology

Index : Biology 57

- Molecular 577.2

577.2 Molecular biology

Problem 113

Textbook of Plant Pathology

Main class : Botany 58

Subclass : Plant diseases 581.2

581.2 Textbook of Plant Pathology

Problem 114

Himalayan Flora

Index : Himalayan region (1-925.36)

Flora 581.9

581.9(1-925.36) Himalayan Flora

Problem 115

Current advances in Cytogenetics

Keywords : Cytology

Genetics

Index : Cytology 576

Cytogenetics 575

575 Current advances in Cytogenetics.

Problem 116

Flora and Fauna of Andhra Pradesh.

Main class : Fauna and Flora (Combined)

Paleontology 56.017.2

Common auxiliaries

of Place : Andhra Pradesh (548.4)

Index : Fauna : 591.9

Flora : 581.9

Fauna & Flora (combined) : 56.017.2

56.017.2(548.4) Flora and Fauna of Andhra Pradesh

5.5 6. APPLIED SCIENCES. MEDICINE. TECHNOLOGY

Problem 117

Feeding by means of a stomach tube

Keywords : Feeding
Stomach tube

Index : Feeding
by stomach tube 613.2.032.33

Main class : Medicine 61

Subclass : Hygiene 613

Subclass : Nutrition 613.2

Special auxiliary subdivision : Feeding by stomach tube .032.33

613.2.032.33 Feeding by stomach tube

Problem 118

Diseases of the Nervous system

Keywords : Nervous system
Diseases

Index : Nervous system 612.8
Diseases
Process 616-092

612.8:616-092 Diseases of the nervous system

Problem 119

Recurrence of tonsilitis

Index : Tonsilitis 616.322-002
Recurrence 616-036.87

Main class : Medicine 61

Subclass : Pathology 616

Subclass : Digestive system 616.3

Subdivision : Pharynx 616.32

Subdivision : Tonsils 616.322

Special auxiliary
subdivision : Inflammation - 022
Recurrence - 036.87

Medicine - Pathology - Digestive System - Pharynx - Tonsils -
61 616 616.3 616.32 616.322
Inflammation - Recurrence
-022 -036.87

616.322-022-036.87 is the required number

Problem 120

Reliability Engineering

Index : Reliability .004.15
Engineering 62

Main class : Engineering 62

Common auxilaries
Point of view : Reliability .004.15

62.004.15 Reliability Engineering

Problem 121

Advanced materials for Engineers

Index : Materials testing 620.1

Engineering : 62

'Materials' is classified under Engineering class hence no separate class number need be given to Engineering. Therefore,

620.1 Advanced materials for engineers.

Problem 121A

Theory of Nondestructive testing

Index : Non destructive testing 620.179.1

Main class : Engineering

Subclass : Materials testing 620.1

Subclass : Strength tests 620.17

Subdivision : Non destructive testing 620.179.1

620.179.1 Theory of Non destructive Testing.

Problem 122

Engineering fracture mechanics : an international conference proceedings.

Index : Fracture Mechanics 539.42
Engineering 62

62:539.42(063) Engineering fracture mechanics : an international conference proceedings.

Problem 123

Thermal endurance testing of materials.

Keywords : Thermal tests
Endurance tests

Index : Endurance tests 620.169.1
Thermal testing 620.179.13

620.169.1+620.179.13 Here both endurance testing and thermal testing are combined. Hence addition relation.

Problem 124

Corrosion inhibitors : an international conference

Keywords : Corrosion
Inhibitors

Index : Corrosion inhibitors 620.197.3
Proceedings (063)

Main class : Materials testing 620.1

Subclass : Corrosion 620.19

Subclass : Protection of Materials 620.197

Subdivision : Corrosion inhibitors 620.197.3

Common auxiliaries of Form : Proceedings (063)

620.197.3(063) is the required number

Problem 125

Alternative Energy Resources

Keywords : Renewable energy
Alternative energy

Index : Alternative energy 620.92
Sources 62-67

Main class : Energy 620.9

Subclass : Use of alternative energy 620.92

Special auxiliary subdivision : Other energy sources 62-67

620.92-67 Alternative energy sources

Problem 126

Energy resources : a bibliography

Index : Energy resources 620.91
Bibliography (01)

620.91(01) Energy Resources : a bibliography.

Problem 127

Basic Engineering Thermodynamics

Keywords : Engineering
Thermodynamics

Primary Main class : Engineering 62

Secondary Main class : Physics 53

Subclass : Heat 536

Subdivision : Thermodynamics 536.7

62:536.7 Basic Engineering Thermodynamics

Problem 128

Practical servomechanism design

Keywords : Servomechanisms

Index : Servo controls 62-503.54
Design .001.63

Main class : Engineering 62

Subclass : Servo controls 62-503.54

Common auxiliaries
Points of view : Design .001.63

62-503.54.001.63 Practical Servomechanism design

Problem 129

Mechanical design and systems hand book

Keywords : Mechanical Engineering
Hand books

Main class : Mechanical Engineering 621.01

Common auxiliaries
of Form : Handbook (035)

621.01(035) Mechanical design and systems handbook.

Problem 130

Dynamics of Machinery

(Note : The scope of the book is about the characteristics and details of machines)

The title is generally referred to the class Engineering. If we look at 62 class, we find at 62-1/-9 Characteristics and details of machines.

Hence we can select *62-1/-9* for the title Dynamics of Machinery.

Problem 131

Transonic flow problems in Turbomachinery

Keywords : Flow
Transonic flow
Turbomachinery

Index : Turbomachines 621-135
Transonic Flow 533.6.011.35

Primary Main class : Mechanical Engineering 621

Special auxiliary
subdivision : Turbomachines 621-135

Secondary Main class : Physics 53

Subclass : Aerodynamics 533.6

Subdivision : Transonic flow 533.6.011.35

621-135:533.6.011.35 Transonic flow problems in Turbo- machinery

Problem 132

Inst. of Mechanical Engineers Conference on Vibrations in Rotating Machinery.

Index : Rotating machinery 62-25
Vibrations 534.01

Primary Main Class : Engineering 62.

Special auxiliary subdivision : Rotary elements 62-25

Secondary Main Class : Physics 53

Subclass : Acoustics 534

Subdivision : Vibrations 534.01

Common auxiliaries Form : Proceedings (063)

62-25:534.01(063) I. Mech. Engr. conference on vibrations in rotating machinery

Problem 133

Design of modern control systems.

Keywords : Control systems design.

Index : Control systems 681.5
design .001.63

Main Class : Industries. Crafts. Trades 68

Subclass : Precision mechanisms 681

Subdivision : Automatic control engineering 681.5

Common auxiliaries of Points of view : design .001.63

681.5.001.63 Design of modern control systems.

Problem 134

Systems modelling and optimisation.

Index : Modelling
Control Engineering 681.5.015
Optimisation .001.26.

Main class : Industries. Crafts. Trades 62
Subclass : Precision mechanisms 681
Subdivision : Automatic control Engineering 681.5
Subdivision : Modelling 681.5.015
Common auxiliaries Points of view : optimisation. 001.26
681.5.015.001.26 Systems modelling and optimisation.

Problem 135

Theory and problems of feedback control systems
Index : Feedback control systems 681.516.3
Main Class : Precision Mechanisms and instruments 681
Subclass : Automatic control Engg 681.5
Subdivision : Feedback control 681.516.3
Common auxiliaries of Form : Problems and solutions (076.2)

681.516.3(076.2) Theory and problems of feedback control systems

Problem 136

International conference on condition monitoring
Key words : Maintenance
Condition monitoring
Main class : Engineering 62
Special auxiliary subdivision : Maintenance 62-7
Common auxiliary Point of view : Monitoring .001.42
Common auxiliary Form : Proceedings (063)

Here we have to infer from the word condition monitoring that this is something to do with the maintenance, servicing and other preventive measures for the machine to avoid break down. Hence maintenance word is to be selected to look under index.

62-7.001.42(063) International conference on condition monitoring.

Problem 137

Elements of Nuclear reactor design.

Main Class : Nuclear Engineering 621.039

Subclass : Reactor Engineering 621.039.4

621.039.4 Elements of Nuclear reactor design

Problem 138

Steam: its generation and use

Index : Steam
Uses 621.1

Main Class : Engineering 62

Subclass : Mechanical Engineering 621

Subdivision : Generation and use of steam 621.1

621.1 Steam: its generation and use

Problem 139

Advances in steam turbine technology for power generation.

Keywords : Steam turbines
Electric power generation.

Index : Steam turbines 621.165
Electric power generation 621.311

Primary Main Class : Mechanical Engineering 621

Subclass : Steam generation 621.1

Subdivision : Steam turbines 621.165

Secondary Main Class : Electrical Engineering 621.3

Subclass : Power generation and supply 621.311

621.165:621.311 Advances in steam turbine technology for power generation

Problem 140

Current state of technology in hydraulic machines.

Keywords : Hydraulic machines
State-of-the-art.

Index : Hydraulic machinery 621.22
Development work .001.6

Main class : Mechanical Engineering 621

Subclass : Hydraulic Energy 621.22

Common auxiliaries
Points of view : development. 001.6

621.22.001.6 Developments in hydraulic machinery
(State of the art technology in hydraulic machinery)

Problem 141

Audels Power plant guide

Keywords : Power plants
Guidebooks

Main class : Electrical Engineering 621.3

Subclass : Electric Power generation 621.311

Common
auxiliaries Form : Guidebooks (036)

621.311(036) Audels Power plant guide.

Problem 142

High voltage Engineering and testing

Keywords : Electrical Engineering. High Voltage testing

Index : High voltage 621.3.027.3
Testing .001.4

Main Class : Electrical Engg. 621.3

Subclass : High Voltage 621.3.027.3
(Special auxiliary subdivision.027.3)

Common auxiliary
Points of view : Testing .001.4

621.3.027.3.001.4 High Voltage Engineering testing.

Problem 143

Power Plant Performance

Keywords : Electric Power generation
Power Plants
Performance.

Index : Electric Power generation 621.311
Power Stations 621.311.2
Performance: 621.311.2.004.15

Main Class : Electrical Engineering 621.3

Subclass : Electrical Power generation 621.311

Subdivision : Power stations 621.311.2

Common auxiliaries
of Points of view : Performance .004.15

621.311.2.004.15 Power Plant Performance.

Problem 144

Proceedings of American Power conference.

Keywords : Electric Power generation.

Main Class : Electrical Engineering 621.3

Subclass : Electric Power generation 621.311

Common auxiliaries
of Form : Proceedings (063)

621.311(063) Proceedings of American Power conference

Problem 145

Seminar on steam and gas based cogeneration systems.

Keywords : Steam Plants
Gas Plants
Electric Power generation
Cogeneration.

Index : Power Stations using steam
621.311.22

Power Stations using gaseous fuels 621.311.22-62.

Here power stations use both steam and gas combined for generating power.

621.311.22-62(063) Seminar on steam and gas based cogeneration systems.

Problem 146

Refurbishment of Power station electrical plant

Keywords	:	Power Stations
		Power Plants
		Retrofitting
Index	:	Power plants 621.311.2
		Renovation .004.69
Main Class	:	Electrical Engineering 621.3
Subclass	:	Electric Power generation 621.311
SubDivision	:	Power Plants 621.311.2
Common auxiliaries of Points of view	:	Renovation .004.69

621.311.2.004.69 Refurbishment of Power Station Electrical plant.

Problem 147

Energy Efficient electric motors and their applications.

Keywords	:	Electric motors
		Energy efficiency
Index	:	Electric motors 621.313.13
		Energy efficiency 621.3.017
Main Class	:	Electrical engineering 621.3
Subclass	:	Electrical Machines 621.313
Subdivision	:	Electric Motors 621.313.13
Special auxiliary subdivision	:	Energy Efficiency 621.3.017

621.313.13.017 Energy Efficiency Electric motors

Problem 148

Electric Power distribution system.

Keywords : Electric Power distribution

Index : Distribution
electricity 621.316.1

Main Class : Electrical Engineering 621.3

Subclass : Distribution and regulation
of electrical energy 621.316

Subdivision : Distribution networks 621.316.1

621.316.1 Electric Power distribution system.

Problem 149

International conference on Electrical Insulation and dielectrics.

Keywords : Electrical insulation
Dielectrics

Index : Dielectrics 537.226
Dielectric Materials 621.315.61
Electrical insulation materials
621.315.61

This book deals with materials related to dielectrics and electrical insulation. Therefore, we have to select 621.315.61 which is analysed as follows.

Main Class : Electrical Engineering 621.3

Subclass : Transmission of electrical energy
621.315

Subdivision : Insulating materials
dielectric materials 621.315.61

Common auxilia-
ries of Form : Proceedings (063)

621.315.61(063) International Conference on Electrical insulation and dielectrics.

Problem 150

ASME/IEEE Railroad conference

Keywords : Railroads
Railway electrification

Primary Main Class : Electrical Engineering 621.3

Subclass : Electric traction 621.33

Secondary Main Class : Railway engineering 625.1

621.33:625.1(063) is the required number.

Problem 151

Designing with operational amplifiers.

Keywords : Amplifiers
Operations
design.

Index : Amplifiers 621.375
Operational point of view .004

Main Class : Electrical Engineering 621.3

Subclass : Electromagnetic Waves 621.37

Subdivision : Amplifiers 621.375

Common auxiliaries
Point of view : Operations .004

621.375.004 is the required number.

Problem 152

Piping systems drafting and design.

Keywords : Piping
Drafting

Index : Pipes 621.643.2
Piping 621.774
Drawing 621.774.7

Main Class : Mechanical Engineering 621

Subclass : Mechanical Technology 621.7

Subclass : Rolling, extruding, drawing 621.77

Subdivision : Tube and Pipe manufacture 621.774

Subdivision : Drawing down, expanding of Pipe 621.774.7

621.774.7 Piping systems drawing.

Problem 153

Bulk solids handling

Keywords : Material handling
Solids
Bulk materials

Index : Bulk material 62-405.6
Machine elements 621.8
Materials Handling 621.86

Main Class : Mechanical Engineering 621.8

Subclass : Machine elements 621.8

Subdivision : Materials Handling 621.86

Special auxiliary subdivision : Bulk material 62-405.6

621.86-405.6 Bulk materials handling (solids)

Problem 154

Matrix structural analysis.

Keywords : Matrix analysis
Structural Engineering

Index : Matrix analysis 519.612
Structural engineering 624
Structural design 624.04

Primary Main Class : Civil Engineering 624

Subclass : Structural design 624.04

Secondary Main class : Mathematics 51

Subclass : Combinatorial analysis 519.1

Subdivision : Matrix solutions 519.612

624.04:519.612 Matrix structural analysis

Problem 155

Air pollution control equipment

Keywords : Air Pollution
Pollution Control

Index : Air Pollution control 614.7
Equipment .005

Main Class : Medicine 61

Subclass : Public Health. Hygiene 614

Subdivision : Pollution Control 614.7

Common auxiliaries

Points of view : Equipment .005

614.7.005 Air pollution control equipment

Problem 156

Principles of desalination

Keyword : Desalination

Index : Desalination (Water) 628.165

Main Class : Engineering 62

Subclass : Public Health Engineering 628

Subdivision : Water treatment 628.16

Subdivision : Water desalination 628.165

628.165 Principles of desalination.

Problem 157

Modern Production management

Keyword : Production management.

Index : Production Management 658.5

Main Class : Management 65

Subclass : Industrial management 658

Subdivision : Production management 658.5

658.5 Modern Production Management

Problem 158

Mechanical design of Heat exchangers.

Keywords : Heat exchangers

Mechanical design.

Index : Heat exchangers 66.045.1

Mechanical design .001.63

Main Class : Chemical Technology 66

Subdivision : Heat exchangers 66.045.1

Common auxiliaries

Points of view : design .001.63

66.045.1.001.63 Mechanical design of Heat exchangers.

Problem 159

Coal gasification

Keyword : Coal Gasification

Index : Coal gas, fuel technology 662.764

Main Class : Chemical Technology 66

Subclass : Fuels 662

Subclass : Fuel Technology 662.7

Subdivision : Gaseous fuels 662.76

Subdivision : Coal gasification 662.764

662.764 Coal gasification

Problem 160

Electrical Engineering problems in pulp and paper industry

Keywords : Pulp and paper

Electrical Engineering

Index : Pulp and paper technology 676

Electrical Engineering 621.3

Primary Main Class : Pulp and Paper Technology 676

Secondary Main

Class : Electrical Engineering

676;621.3 Electrical Engineering Problems in Pulp and Paper industry.

Problem 161

IEEE Conference on Electrical Engineering problems in Rubber and Plastics industry.

Keywords : Electrical Engineering
Rubber and Plastics
Primary Main Class : Rubber and Plastics industry 678
Secondary Main Class : Electrical Engineering 621.3
Common auxiliaries of Form : Proceedings (063)

678:621.3(063) is the required number.

Problem 162

Thermal spray coatings

Keywords : Thermal spraying. coatings.
Index : Coatings Metal 669.058
Spray coating 621.793.79
Primary Main Class : Metallurgy 669
Subclass : Coating 669.058
Secondary Main Class : Mechanical Engineering 621
Subclass : Workshop Technology 621.7
Subdivision : Metal Coating 621.793
Subdivision : Spray coating 621.793.79

669.058:621.793.79 Thermal spray coating

Problem 163

Theory and problems of data structures

Keywords : Data structure
Solutions
Index : Data design 681.3.02
Solutions (076.2)
Main Class : Precision mechanism 681

Sub Class : Computers 681.3

Subdivision : design of data 681.3.02

Common auxiliaries
of Form : Solutions (076.2)

681.3.02(076.2) Theory and problems of Data Structures

Problem 164

Handbook of Electronic data processing

Keywords : Data processing
Handbooks

Index : Data processing principles 681.3.01
Handbooks (035)

Main Class : Precision Mechanisms 681

Subclass : Computers 681.3

Subdivision : Data processing 681.3.01

Common auxiliaries
of Form : Handbooks (035)

681.3.01(035) Handbook of Electronic data processing

Problem 165

Computer programming in UNIX.

Keywords : Computer programming
Programming languages

Index : Computer Programming 681.3.06
Programming languages 681.3.062

Main Class : Precision Mechanism 681

Subclass : Computers 681.3

Subdivision : Computer Software 681.3.06

Subdivision : Computer Languages 681.3.062

Direct alphabetical specification

(Table 1b) : Unix Computer language

681.3.062UNIX Computer programming in UNIX

Problem 166

Dbase IV User manual

Keyword : Programming languages
User manuals

Index : Programming languages 681.3.062
Manuals - instructions (083.133)

Main Class : Precision mechanisms 681

Subclass : Computers 681.3

Subdivision : Computer Software 681.3.06

Subdivision : Computer languages 681.3.062

Alphabetization device : Dbase IV 681.3.062 dbIV

Common auxiliaries of Form : instruction manuals (083.133)

681.3.062dbIV(083.133) Dbase IV User manual

Problem 167

Sensors and actuators :

Index : Sensors 681.586
Actuators 681.587

Main Class : Precision Mechanisms 681

Subclass : Automatic Control 681.568

Subdivision : Components 681.58

Subdivision : Sensors 681.586
Actuators 681.587

681.586/.587 Sensors and actuators, (Sensors and actuators have consecutive numbers 681.586 and 681.587 respectively. Hence / (extension sign) is used)

Problem 168

Digital computer fundamentals

Keyword : Digital Computers

Index : Digital Computers 681.32

Main Class : Precision Mechanisms 681
Subclass : Computers 681.3
Subdivision : Digital Computers 681.32
681.32 Digital Computer fundamentals.

Problem 169

Furniture upholstery work
Keyword : Furniture
Upholstery
Index : Furniture 684
Upholstery 684.73
Main Class : Industries. Crafts. Trades 68
Subclass : Furniture 684
Subdivision : Upholstery 684.73
684.73 Furniture Upholstery Work

Problem 170

Air conditioning plant and Machinery
Keywords : Air conditioning
Plant and Machinery
Index : Air conditioning 697.9
Plant and Machinery 697.912
697.912 Air conditioning Plant and Machinery

5.6 7:ARTS. RECREATION. SPORTS.

Problem 171

Landscape Planning
Index : Landscape Planning 712
Main Class : Arts 7
Subclass : Physical Planning 71
Subdivision : Landscape Planning 712
712 Landscape Planning

Problem 172

Architecture of Railway stations.

Keywords : Architecture
Railway stations

Index : Architecture 72
Railway Stations 725.31

Main Class : Arts 7

Subclass : Architecture 72

Subdivision : Public architecture 725

Subdivision : Railway stations 725.31

725.31 Architecture of Railway Stations.

Problem 173

Decorative tiles for home interiors

Keywords : Tiles
Decorative tiles
Home interiors

Index : Decorative tiles 738.81
Interior decoration 747

Primary Main Class : Arts 7
Subclass : Plastic Arts 73
Subdivision : Pottery 738
Subdivision : Decorative tiles 738.81

Secondary Main
Class : Arts 7
Subclass : Drawing 74
Interior decoration 747

738.81:747 Decorative tiles for home interiors.

Problem 174

Techniques of engineering drawing

Keywords : Engineering
Drawing
Technical drawing

Main Class : Arts. 7
Subclass : Drawing 74
Subclass : Technical drawing 744
744 Techniques of Engineering drawing

Problem 175

Paintings of the Mughal period.
Keyword : Paintings
Mughal period.
Index : Paintings 75
Mughal period 954.02
(Indian history)
Primary Main Class : Arts
Subclass : Painting 75
Secondary Main
Class : Geography 9
Subclass : History of Asia 95
Subdivision : History of India 954
Subdivision : Mughal period 954.02
75:954.02 Paintings of the Mughal period

Problem 176

Techniques of Lithography
Index : Lithography 763
Mainclass : Arts 7
Subclass : Graphic Arts 76
Subdivision : Planographic techniques 763
763 Techniques of Lithography.

Problem 177

Principles of Microfilming
Keywords : Micrography
Microfilming

Index : Microform
Reprography 778.14
Microfilms 778.14.072

Main Class : Arts 7

Subclass : Photography 77

Subclass : Special applications 778

Subdivision : Microcopying 778.14
Microfilms 778.14.072

778.14.072 Principles of Microfilming.

Problem 178

Indian National Anthem

Keywords : National anthem
India

Index ; National anthems 784.71
India (540)

Main Class : Arts 7

Subclass : Music 78

Subdivision : Vocal Music 784

Subdivision : National anthems 784.71

Common auxiliaries
of Place : India (540)

784.71(540) Indian National anthem.

Problem 179

Musical direction of grand opera

Keywords : Music
Direction
Grand Opera

Index : Musical direction 792.027.4
Opera 792.545

Main Class : Arts 7

Subclass : Recreation 79
Subclass : Theatre 792
Subdivision : Opera 792.545
Special auxiliary
subdivision : Musical direction 792.027.4

792.545.027.4 Musical direction of grand opera

Problem 180:

42 Kilometer flat event, Marathon racing

Keywords : Running
Sports events
Index : Running
Athletics 796.422
Distances 796.093.3
Long distance
running 796.422.16
Main Class : Arts 7
Subclass : Recreation 79
Subclass : Sports 796
Subdivision : Athletics 796.42
Subdivision : Running 796.422
Sub division : Long distance 796.422.16
Special auxiliary
subdivision : Distance. Course 796.093.3
subdivision
: specify distance by adding (181...)

Here the distance is 42km flat event

Therefore, 796.093.3 (181km 42) is 42km flat event.

796.422.16.093.3(181km42) 42 Kilometer flat event, Marathon racing.

5.7 8. LANGUAGE. LINGUISTICS. LITERATURE

Problem 181

English Etymological dictionary

Keywords : English

Etymology
dictionary

Index : English language 811.111
Etymology (lexicology) 81 '373.6
Etymological dictionary 81'374.4

Main Class : Linguistics and Language. Literature 8

Subclass : Language 811

Subdivision : English 811.111

Special auxiliary subdivision : Etymology 81'373.6

Special auxiliary subdivision : Etymological dictionary 81'374.4

811.111'374.4 English Etymological dictionary

Problem 182

Telugu literary works of 18th century

Keywords : Telugu Literature
18th century

Main Class : Linguistics, Literature 8

Subclass : Literature 82

Subdivision : Telugu literature 821.572.24

Common auxiliaries of Time : 18th century "17"

Common auxiliaries of Form : Collection (081.1)

821.572.24"17"(081.1) Telugu literary works of 18th century

Problem 183

Kalidasa's works.

Keywords : Sanskrit literature
Kalidasa
Literary works

Index : Sanskrit Literature 821.211
Main Class : Language, Literature 8
Subclass : Literature 82
Subclass : Literature of individual languages 821
Subdivision : Sanskrit Literature 821.211
Alphabetization device : Kalidasa's works 821.211KAL

821.211KAL Kalidasa's works.

Problem 184

Anda lusiam dialect of Spanish

Keywords : Language
dialect
Spanish
Index : Dialects 81'282
Spanish language 811.134.2
Main Class : Language, Literature 8
Subclass : Language and Linguistics 81
Subclass : Languages 811
Subdivision : Romance Languages 811.13
Subdivision : Spanish 811.134.2
Special auxiliary subdivision : dialects 81'282
Subdivision : Regional dialects 81'282.3
Common auxiliary Place : Andalucia (468.1)

811.134.2'282.3(468.1) is the required number.

Problem 185

Language of Polish school children.

Keywords : Languages
Poland
School children

Index : Polish Language 811.162.1
School children - 053.5

Main Class : Language, Literature 8

Subclass : Language 811

Subdivision : Polish language 811.162.1

Special auxiliary subdivision : Usage of language 81'276

Subdivision : Language of Particular age group 81'276.3

Common auxiliaries of Persons : School children -053.5

811.162.1'276.3-053.5 Language of Polish school children.

Problem 186

Machine translation.

Keywords : Translation
Computers

Index : Machine translation 81'322.4

Main Class : Language, Literature 8

Subclass : Language 81

Special auxiliary subdivision : Mathematical Linguistics 81'32
Computational Linguistics 81'322

Subdivision : Machine translation 81'322.4

81'322.4 Machine translation

Problem 187

Criticism of German dramatic works in English

Keywords : German Literature
Drama
Criticism

Index : German Literature 821.112.2

Drama 82-2
Literary criticism 82.09
English = 111

Main Class : Language, Literature 8
Subclass : Literature 82
Subdivision : German Literature 821.112.2
Special auxiliary subdivision : Drama 82-2
Special auxiliary subdivision : Literary criticism 82.09

821.112.2-2.09 Criticism of German dramatic works

Problem 188

Art of Public speaking

Keyword : Public speaking
Index : Public speaking 82.085.2
Main Class : Literature 82
Subdivision : Rhetoric 82.085
Subdivision : Speaking 82.085.2

82.085.2 Art of Public speaking

Problem 189

Art of Literary writing

Keywords : Writing
Literature
Index : Writing
Literary technique 82.081
Main Class : Literature 82
Subdivision : Literary activity 82.08
Subdivision : Creative writing 82.081

82.081 Art of Literary writing

Problem 190

The Tamil alphabet

Keywords : Tamil
Alphabet

Index : Language 81
Languages 811
Tamil =573.15
Alphabet 81'351
Main Class : Language, Literature 8
Subclass : Language 81
Subclass : Languages 811
Subdivision : Tamil 811.573.15
Special auxiliary subdivision : Alphabet 81'351

811.573.15'351 The Tamil alphabet

5.8 9. GEOGRAPHY. BIOGRAPHY. HISTORY

Problem 191

Geographical exploration of Glaciers

Keywords : Exploration
Geography
Glaciers
Index : Exploration 910
Glaciology 551.32
Primary Main Class : Geography, Biography, History 9
Subclass : Exploration, Travel 910
Subdivision : Exploration of particular geographical features 910.3
Secondary Main Class : Sciences 5
Subclass : Earth science 55
Subclass : Geology 551
Subdivision : External geodynamics 551.3
Subdivision : Glaciology 551.32
Subdivision : Glaciers 551.324

910.3:551.324 Geographical exploration of Glaciers

Problem 192

Studies on Romania

Keywords : Romania
Geographical studies

Index : Romania (498)
Area studies 908

Main Class : Geography, Biography, History 9

Subclass : Area studies 908

Subdivision : Area studies Romania 908.498

908.498 Studies on Romania

Problem 193

History of ancient China

Keywords : History
China

Index : History 93
China ancient (315)

Main Class : Geography, Biography, History 9

Subclass : History 93
Ancient history 931

Subdivision : History of ancient China 931.5

931.5 History of ancient China.

Problem 194

Biography of Jawaharlal Nehru.

Index : Biography 929

Main Class : Geography, Biography, History 9

Subclass : Biography 929

Alphabetical device : Jawaharlal Nehru 929 Jawaharlal

929 Jawaharlal Biography of Jawaharlal Nehru.

Problem 195

History of the Polar regions.

Index : Polar regions
History 990

Main Class : Geography, Biography, History 9

Subclass : History 93/99

Subdivision : History of Polar regions 990

990 History of Polar regions.

Problem 196

International Who's Who.

Keyword : Biography

Index : Biography 929
International (100)

Main Class : Geography, Biography, History 9

Subclass : Biographies 929

Common auxiliaries
of Place : International (100)

929(100) International Who's Who.

Problem 197

History of British India.

Index : History
British India 954.03

Main Class : Geography, Biography, History 9

Subclass : Medieval history 94

Subdivision : British India 954.03

954.03 History of British India.

Problem 198

Indian National flag

Keywords : National flags
India

Index : National flags 929.921
India (540)

Main Class : Geography, Biography, History 9

Subclass : Biographical and related studies

Subdivision : Flags 929.9

Subdivision : National flags 929.921

Common auxiliaries
of Place : India (540)

929.921(540) Indian National flag

Problem 199

Travel between India and Sri Lanka

Keywords : Travels
India
Sri Lanka

Index : Travels 910.4
India (540)
Sri Lanka (548.7)

Main Class : Geography, Biography, History 9

Subclass : Geography 910

Subdivision : Travels 910.4

Common auxiliaries
of Place : India (540)

Common auxiliaries
of Place : Sri Lanka (548.7)

910.4(540:548.7) Travel between India and Sri Lanka

Problem 200

Urban agglomeration in India during 19th Century.

Keywords : Urban settlement
India
19th century

Index : Urban settlements 911.374.6
911.375
India (540)
19th Century "18"

Main Class : Geography, Biography, History 9

Subclass : Geography 91

Subclass : General geography 911

Subdivision : Human geography 911.3

Subdivision : Settlements 911.37

Subdivision : Urban settlements 911.375

Common auxiliaries of Place : India (540)

Common auxiliaries of Time : 19th Century "18"

911.375(540)"18" Urban agglomeration in India during 19th Century.

Index